Reader comments on Unwitting Mystic:

"I was dumbfounded by how unthinkably vast your knowing is. I kept having to stop reading for a moment to take in the words, and sometimes just to cry because it is so clear you know. You really know what most of us only try to believe." Tenzin P., Himachal Pradesh, India

"I truly have been rattled to the core in such a way that words can't describe." Lorraine C., New Mexico, USA

"I am in awe. I loved every word." Kate L., Idaho, USA

"It feels like another light has been brightly illuminated in the world." Ann L., Michigan, USA

"I laughed, I cried, and said 'yes, yes, yes' more times than I could count." Helen W., Reading, England

"From beginning to end it has opened my heart." Pepper K., Louisiana, USA

"[The] book is a great spiritual beauty." Beatriz B., Madrid, Spain

"I felt your words and your heart powerfully on so many levels, felt your pain, your frustration, your confusion, your awe and gratitude, your deep mission to serve, and most of all, your love." Holly B., North Carolina, USA

"You have moved me to tears with your words, I'm absolutely blown away by what I read...so honest and raw, and true for us all in some way." Angela P., Arizona, USA

ISBN: 978-1500124908

Unwitting Mystic:

Evolution of The Message of Love

By Mary Reed

To Connie
Big love,
Mary

This book is dedicated to Margery Silverton.

Thank you for my life.

CONTENTS

Part 1

Why, if it was an illusion, not praise the catastrophe, whatever it was, that destroyed illusion and put truth in its place?

~Virginia Woolf, *A Room of One's Own*

Chapter 1

It is 2:00 PM on Wednesday, March 23, 2011. Mist from a passing rain lingers outside my second floor condominium as ice-gray light reaches through two large living room windows scarcely touching the edge of my dining room. It is noticeably quiet, as though the afternoon is suspended between reflection and anticipation.

Sitting at my polished oak dining table, where Tilda is curled up in a circle beneath my chair, I pick up one of two small Compazine pills lying beside my laptop, place it on my tongue and wash it back with a sip from my second glass of pinot noir. I click "print" on the computer screen, take another sip, and get up to retrieve from the printer the three pages of my Last Will and Testament and the accompanying one-page letter to my loved ones. Easing back into the chair, I sign both documents at the bottom, add the date, and line the pages up neatly against the seam along the center of the table.

I am unexpectedly calm as I sip my wine and click through various e-mail and social networking accounts, reading and deleting any new messages while I watch the minutes tick away on the top corner of the computer screen. After ten minutes I put the other Compazine on my tongue and wash it back with the last splash of wine, then stand and head down the hall to the sunroom. With Tilda at my heels, I spread a wide swath of newspapers across the tan Berber carpet. Bending down I guide Tilda's little ten-pound frame atop the Lifestyle section, then press down lightly on her fluffy white rear end and say, "Honey, this is where you can go until someone can take you outside, okay?"

On the Tao-style sofa table in the living room are select treasures I want my best friend, Reese, to have: the unity mask from South Africa; the shofar from Jerusalem; the antique Christian ritual instrument from Ethiopia; the Cherokee medicine wheel from New Mexico.

On the matching bookshelf are items for my ex-girlfriend, Mary: the leather bound journal with our love notes pasted inside, the title and keys to my car. Beside the bookshelf, for my dear friend Nan, is a full ten-pound bag of dog food and Tilda's green travel bag packed with grooming supplies and a year's worth of flea and tick prevention medicine.

Near the hall closet is a box sealed and addressed to my family. It contains three photo albums, four manila envelopes bulging with photos of memorable moments with family, friends and various celebrities, and three electronic discs digitally chronicling my adventures in America, Europe, the Middle East, Africa and Asia.

I stop in the kitchen to pour another glass of wine and put four days worth of food and water in large dishes on the floor for Tilda, then walk back to the far end of the dining table where three groups of pills I carefully sorted last night lay in small, medium and large circles. Scooping the smallest circle – another Compazine, five Ambiens and two OxyContins – off the table, I toss all the pills in my mouth and swallow them down with generous gulps of wine. It is now 2:15 PM.

I did not know what to expect of this moment, so I am relieved to feel at ease and unhurried as I meander through the condo to turn off the thermostat, unplug the coffee pot, check the locks on the front and back doors, lower the living room window shades, shut down the computer and go pee. I walk casually, as though this is my routine every afternoon.

I return to the table and sweep the second circle of pills – two more Compazines, twenty Ambiens and five OxyContins – into my hand and work half of them into my mouth. These go down easily with several swigs of wine. I put the rest in my mouth and drain the glass. It is now 2:19 PM.

There are sixty pills in the last circle, the entire remaining inventory of all three drugs. Once I get these down it will only be a matter of minutes before my liver, kidneys, central nervous system and heart become overloaded and start shutting down. By that time I will be in a deep sleep.

Since my doctors think I still work with orphans in Africa and they are familiar with my complicated medical history, I had no trouble getting them to refill prescriptions for drugs to enhance sleep and ease pain. They had no reason to suspect I would add these to the unused prescriptions I already had and take them all together today. Last Friday before the trash collectors came I emptied all the pills into plastic baggies and threw out the prescription bottles so there would be no immediate evidence of which drugs I took and where I got them. My doctors are conscientious, caring providers and I pray they never discover I betrayed their trust.

I spent weeks researching the metabolic actions of each drug – which organs they affect, over how long of time, how they all interact – and planned the combinations and timing carefully to avoid throwing up, losing control of my bowels or falling asleep before I have taken all the pills. By now the first Compazine pill is blocking nausea triggers in my gut and brain, and the second pill is starting to kick in as backup. The alcohol is providing a medium in which to more rapidly dissolve and intensify the effects of the Ambien and OxyContin pills. If my research is correct then from the time I ingested the first handful until the start of a deep sleep will only be about eight to ten minutes – somewhere around 2:23 to 2:25 PM. The second batch of drugs I just took will kick in eight to ten minutes from now and put me under even deeper. According to all I have read, this volume of drugs will begin stressing my liver, then my central nervous system, then my kidneys, but will likely not be enough to shut everything down or cause my body to override the Compazine and make me involuntarily vomit. The third batch of drugs will finally kill me. My final breath will likely be sometime before 3:15 PM.

I take my wine glass to the kitchen, wash it and put it in the cabinet, then head into the bathroom to brush my teeth. When I return to the dining table I sweep the remaining sixty pills into both hands and say, "Come on, T-pot," as Tilda follows me into the bedroom and jumps up on the end of the bed. An hour earlier I put clean sheets on my sleek mahogany platform bed, stacked three pillows up at the top on the left side, turned down the covers, and placed a full glass of water on the nightstand. I am already in my favorite green plaid flannel pants and gray cotton t-shirt; all I have to do is take the pills and lie down.

Sitting near the head of the bed I drop the pills onto the white down-filled comforter and pinch about a dozen back up into my left palm. I am conscious of not wanting to fill my bladder more full than necessary so I swallow the first batch with as little water as possible and do the same with each batch until I have all sixty pills down without needing to refill the glass. I check my watch one last time. It is 2:22 PM.

After placing the empty glass back on the nightstand I lie back slightly elevated on the three pillows to lessen the risk of regurgitating any pills. Looking down at the end of the bed I say, "I love you with all my heart, Tilda." These are the last words I will ever speak out loud, and as I hear them drift momentarily in the air I am aware that in the last moments of my life I feel blessed to know there is genuine love present.

Chapter 2

I have always been a kind, good-natured girl. I say hello to strangers, dance with abandon to hokey country music and gleefully invite dogs to kiss me on the lips. For many years people likened my disposition and petite, blonde appearance to the actress Sandy Duncan, who was known to be particularly spunky. Like everyone else I have moments of frustration, of course, but as a rule I can be annoyingly cheerful and I own that comfortably.

At the same time, I have also always been a ruminator, preferring to consider the world intuitively rather than through what I was taught in my two college degrees or what society and history book authors tell me is true.

For the past twenty-two years I have been a kind, good-natured, cheerful ruminator who has had numerous involuntary visions and insights (a sudden embodied 'knowing' or experience). These have occurred in fully awakened states, in meditation, in the stages of semi-alertness just going into or coming out of sleep, and under hypnosis. Since December 2000 all my visions and insights have related solely to God, Jesus, Buddha, angels (beings of light), the origins and evolution of life, and my purpose here on Earth.

For many years these weighty mystical events confused me, to put it mildly, because I did not grow up religious or even remotely interested in spiritual pursuits. I never read the Bible and had no understanding whatsoever of Buddhism until a few years ago when the Dalai Lama gave a teaching in Washington, DC and someone suggested I attend. The closest I came to being religious was living with a Jewish woman for seven years and hosting a fabulous Passover Seder with her and her mother every spring. From a spiritual perspective I never really sought to do anything other than just be a good person, do compassionate work, and eat gefilte fish with gusto once a year.

I did, however, have an inkling when I was a child that humans are capable of accessing much deeper wisdom and compassion than most seemed to realize. I recall one hot Sunday afternoon when I was about seven years old standing in my grandmother's parched front yard in Clovis, New Mexico staring up at the vaporous desert sun and pondering the question of why people go to church to learn about Jesus when he was right in their heart. I touched my dust-speckled yellow cotton blouse at the center of my chest and whispered, "Why can't they hear him in here?"

What prompted this pondering was the constant judgment and damnation I kept hearing from all the self-proclaimed Christians I knew. On the day of my quiet questioning there must have been a particularly fiery sermon at Parkland Baptist Church, because the distance between Aunt Irma's car door and Gran Gran's front door was not nearly enough to hold all the shaming those two were dishing out about fellow churchgoers with whom they had just shared every stanza of *Amazing Grace*.

The Jesus people were finding in church was not the same Jesus I had in my heart. Mine was always, without exception, kind, compassionate and unconditionally loving of everyone equally. Church Jesus seemed to love only on condition and was evidently quite peeved at all the sinning still going on even after he had given his life for said sins.

Instinctively I mistrusted Church Jesus. And despite my valiant efforts to stay tuned in, the steady drip of damnatory chatter that seeped into my awareness through family, friends, neighbors, teachers, books, radio and television eventually drowned out the Jesus in my heart.

That is, until I was given sight into the Divine world.

It started in the summer of 2000. I heard a voice deep in the recesses of my mind say, "You are supposed to be doing something *very* important." The voice did not have a tone normally associated with human speech. It was much deeper, like the after-sound vibration one senses momentarily when a bass singer hits a low note. At the time this happened I lived in Washington, DC and was crisscrossing the country directing national clinical research programs in respiratory medicine. I was already doing something I considered important, and that work kept me far too busy to heed the call of a phantom voice.

But the voice would not be denied. I began hearing it on airplanes, in elevators, in meetings, during meals and countless other random moments, and every time it said the same thing: "You are supposed to be doing something *very* important." The more I tried to ignore it the more persistent it became.

Six months after the voice started I was running on the beach at sunrise on Amelia Island in Florida and going over in my mind a talk I was to give that day. Suddenly, and with such force I had to stop right where I was, it occurred to me I had forgotten something extremely important. Inexplicably, I understood that either I had come into this world with important information and forgotten it over the years, or I had forgotten to bring the important information into this world with me in the first place. Neither possibility made sense to me since I had never entertained the idea of any kind of life before or after the one I was living. To intentionally bring information in or leave information behind meant I had to have been in some kind of life before this one.

Given the persistence of the voice and now this new forceful realization, I accepted that I was going to have to figure out what was going on. When I returned to DC I called my friend Sue, a psychotherapist in Arkansas who was well versed in otherworldly phenomena given that she had endured a near-death experience after an auto accident and held a Ph.D. in transcendental psychology. I told her everything and without hesitation she said, "It makes perfect sense to me. I would be glad to help."

I flew to Arkansas at the end of the week and spent nearly seven hours that Saturday and Sunday deeply immersed in a world that would turn everything I thought I knew on its head. And I had entered that world nailed to a cross.

Chapter 3

Reese is expecting me for dinner at Mi Rancho at 6:00 PM. Nearly every Wednesday night for eight years I have met various friends at the same restaurant; for the past two years it has usually been Reese, joined occasionally by Nan, sometimes other friends and Mary when she is in town.

Reese will worry when I do not show up. She will call and text and wonder if perhaps I cancelled and she did not get the message. Since she takes a bus from downtown to the suburbs to meet me on these nights I always give her a ride home. She will probably take a taxi home tonight after eating alone, and in my planning I had to balance my guilt over this with my worry that Tilda could possibly be left alone for days on end. For Tilda's sake I need Reese to suspect something is wrong sooner rather than later.

Tomorrow she will call again. Mary will also call, probably once in the morning and once in the evening as usual. Nan may call as well to see if I want to play golf. At some point one of them will call the other to see if anyone has heard from me, and when they all realize I did not make it to dinner and no one can reach me, they will worry. By Friday, Saturday at the latest, someone will drop by or have the police come to check on me. I desperately do not want any friends to see me dead, for I love them with all my heart and dread the idea of inflicting such trauma. At the same time, I believe only they will likely understand my decision and be able to see me with the mercy of compassion.

I close my eyes and think, intentionally, about forgiveness. Some say our purpose in life is to learn to forgive; at times I believed this was true, at other times I believed this singular purpose to be too narrow. Regardless, I believe it is vital to a peaceful soul so I make sure it is the last thing on my mind.

"Dear God, please forgive me if what I am doing is wrong," I say with my thoughts, pushing the words through my mind with force hoping to illuminate them somehow and extend their reach. "You know the goodness that fills my heart, you know my intentions. If I am mistaken please forgive me, show mercy and help me see the truth." I stop, think for a moment, then add, "I pray also for forgiveness for any hurt I have ever caused another being. I am truly sorry for any moment of pain I brought into this world."

When I can think of nothing else to add I say "Amen" out loud and unclasp my hands to let them rest slack over my chest. A thick tingling has already begun to swirl in my head, and I notice now a warm current rising up from my back into my torso. I feel comforted, truly at peace in knowing I have done my very best to participate in, and now exit, this earth with kind and loving intention. I have been far from perfect, but I did my best. From here it is up to God.

***

At 2:56 PM I am deep into my eternal sleep, surely approaching death, and unaware that Reese is leaving a message on my cell phone letting me know she cannot make it to dinner tonight. She adds that she looks forward to seeing me next week and may give me a call over the weekend to see what I am up to.

Chapter 4

It is Saturday, December 16, 2000. I am lying deeply relaxed on a padded leather table. Sue has slowly counted backwards from ten to zero, and with my eyes closed I have just seen gray smoke rise from the center of my body and become an image of a large golden book lying open on a pedestal. This is followed forcefully by an image of the word "WORDS." The book is of extreme importance. I understand that the words in the book are mine and I am to clarify and tell the truth of these words because what is recorded was incomplete, incorrect or has been misconstrued.

Sue now guides me into a crystal cave. The pathway is narrow in places and I run my hands along the walls for support occasionally as I make my way toward a small light at the far end. I walk all the way to the edge of an opening at the back of the cave, beyond which there is only light. As I step across the threshold into the light, Sue says, "Look down and tell me what you have on your feet."

At first I cannot see my feet because I am what seems to be something akin to a transparent wisp of air. I say, "I can't see my feet. I'm floating, like a spirit or something."

Sue patiently tells me to step back into the cave and slowly step out again. "Can you see your feet now?"

I look down, hesitate, and with some confusion say, "My feet... are nailed to a board."

I become aware now that I am in Jesus at his moment of

physical death. My feet are nailed to a long piece of thick wood. With my arms outstretched, my hands are nailed to a shorter piece of wood. My head is heavy and bobs in surrender to the weight. This cross upon which my body hangs is being dragged sideways along a dirt path leading into a courtyard. The path and courtyard are crowded with loud, highly emotional people.

In this body/mind/spirit I know everything that has happened in the evolution of Man over untold millennia in the past, and I see in great detail all that led to this moment. My death is not the result of a betrayal by a disciple or the ploys of a few people in power who feel threatened by my presence. It is instead caused by a mindset that took ages to cultivate, perpetuate and entrench. In the absence of widespread connection to the flow of God's Love, it is a mindset of conflict and fear that has thrived in the moralizing, domineering egos ruling politics and religion and in the subservient masses at their mercy.

I am filled with immense sadness that so many people will suffer and feel sorrowful because of my death, and my deepest concern and compassion is for those whose actions bring about the events of today. I look out at the emotional crowd and say to myself, "These people do not need to feel sorrowful. They just do not know."

I take my last breath now and feel my spirit pulled up through my chest as though it is being powerfully sucked out. I break free from physical constraints and hover horizontally in spirit form over the shell of my body. No one knows I am still here.

Now in fine, intimate detail I know the emotions present in the heart of every person in the crowd as though they are my own. I know who is filled with shock, who is filled with anger, terror, guilt, rage, grief, sadness, and so on. The vibrations of their grief and guilt are magnificently strong. In every heart, regardless of any other emotions of the moment, there is sorrow. I see this sorrow like a thread stretching from long before this day up through the hearts of all these people and far into the future, all the way into the hearts of current-day humans. The source of this sorrow is the separation from God's Love. Today will allow this sorrow to continue.

I say, "I need to ease these people's sorrows. I never did." And then I say, "This was to have been the point of reconciliation."

In a flurry of activity, I now see what happens in the future. I see quick and vast exploitations of my death. I watch bishops and cardinals and kings scrambling to carve out dominions in my name century after century. I watch countless genuinely well-intentioned people swallowed up in the very same mindset that caused my death, dutifully using my death as instructed by others to further perpetuate separation and conflict with the wedges of guilt, judgment and sin. I see death and more death throughout the centuries in passionate defense of misconstrued understandings of my teachings.

The next thing I am aware of is myself still as Jesus

standing in front of a large golden Bible, which I realize is the same book that appeared to me earlier. I am wearing a white robe made of thick material and my arms are outstretched with palms up. In front of me are people from the crowd who witnessed my death. They are all looking at me expectantly.

"They're listening to me," I say. "They are all listening to me. I need to articulate the reasons, the understanding... you don't have them all, and that is what I need to give them. That's what they are waiting for. That is all they need."

I, as Mary, understand that in my current human form I am not able to give the people what they need yet because in this lifetime I have not yet gotten to a place of perfect love and wisdom. I distinctly feel energy move between my stomach, heart and throat, and say with a slight force as though another being is speaking instructively through me, "The information is yet to come. It is not at this time and place; it is from that place (meaning the Divine world) that I need to give it. It is a completely different place, and it does not come from the shell of these people – of no person."

I feel the energy move inside me again and I clearly see that discovering the information that is yet to come is a journey unto itself and that this journey is to be understood and shared with others. I am also to understand "that place" and bring it together with this earthly world to help everyone understand en masse.

I breathe in deeply and let out a long sigh. "This is enough for today," I say with a tone of finality, and begin to blink.

I have been with? in? as? Jesus for more than three hours and am extremely tired. As I become aware of my body and my surroundings, the solemn emotional remnants of this experience feel like heavy gel draped over my bones, pressing me against the table. I momentarily try to discern whether I am cozy or numb. Before I can make that discernment countless questions flood my mind on a wave of exhilaration. I close my eyes again and take a deep breath. All I want to do is go to sleep and either return to where I just came from or not wake up until I can understand what just happened.

Chapter 5

There is a luxurious, enveloping awareness of love, peace and joy in the realm of angels. The *purity* of each emotion is felt physically, soaking deeply into and engorging one's entire being. The angels communicate kindly, directly, without words. They are happy, laughing, supremely welcoming and witty. They are formless, floating. There is no sense of time with them, no sense of conflict, no sense of awkwardness in being in each other's presence. Being with them is the state of feeling natural and whole in its purest form.

I know these beings and the Divine dimensions as surely as I have ever known anything. In this place is where I feel most at home, most real, most complete. And this is where I expect to be now. But I am not.

The first thing I am aware of is a searing pain emanating from below my ribs on my right side. I am leaden and feel thickly distended as though syrup fills my body so full as to stretch my skin. I push my eyes open with what feels like enormous force, though my eyelids only lift a fraction. I turn my head slowly to the left in small, uncoordinated tics and see the blurry outline of Tilda curled up near my shoulder. I cannot turn my body; the pain is too overwhelming. I blink several times trying to get oriented, my eyelids going down and coming back up slowly as if I am under water. It appears to be nighttime; the shades in my bedroom are down and I cannot make out any light around their edges. My eyeballs feel sunken too deeply in their sockets. I cannot focus enough to see the time on the bedside clock and I cannot lift my arm up to try to see the digital numbers on my watch. I turn my head back awkwardly, close my eyes and breathe in slow, shallow breaths.

The next time I wake up the muscles in my neck, back, stomach, arms, legs and feet are seizing severely. My right side is so taut I am certain it is going to explode. I have to pee, and I can feel pressure on my bladder from internal swelling or cramping in my lower abdomen, I cannot tell which. I blink hard several times, squeezing my eyes together and clenching my teeth against the pain. Shortly I catch a wisp of coherence as it flutters up briefly between the flashes of light streaking through my head and I begin to breathe in slowly through my nose trying to relax and lessen resistance against the various sources of torment. It does not help. I can do nothing but breathe and wait.

It is either just becoming daylight or just becoming dark. The light hanging motionless around the window shades is indistinct, gray. Very slowly, as though bobbing to the surface of my consciousness with a weight still attached, the realization occurs to me that I am still in my same life. My next realization is that I am not so much disappointed as I am shocked. I try to remember – did I get all ninety-seven pills down? Yes, yes, I'm sure I did. I strain to lift my right hand and work against the profuse cramping and sharp stiffness in my arm to bend my elbow and bring my hand sloppily to my mouth, then to my chin, then to my chest to check for vomit. Nothing. "Wow," I say in a hoarse whisper and let my arm drop back by my side.

With my eyes closed I dig for any dregs of strength I can gather beneath my pain, then pray into the viscous milieu of my head, "Please God. Please show me the way. You can see I have no idea what I am doing."

I do not know how many minutes or hours pass before I am able to turn my neck and focus my eyes on the clock. It reads: 8:38. I cannot think clearly enough to understand what that means. I work the numbers around in my head searching for a groove of lucidity to drop them into, but can find none.

Untold hours pass before my muscles stop seizing in unison; now my shoulders, low back, calves and shins rebel in turns but the duration of each cramp is gradually decreasing. My right side feels as if a studded balloon is overinflated under my ribs and is protruding up, down and across my abdominal cavity. I can wait no longer to pee, so I strain with all the force I can muster to pull my legs over the edge of the bed and push my upper body to a seated position. The long Malaysian tapestry on the wall beside my bed waves like a sheet pinned to a clothesline on a breezy day. The large body of water inside my head sloshes heavily to one side then back the other way, then back and forth and back and forth until finally it reaches equilibrium. I push myself up and fall against the wall.

I seem unable to control my movements with instruction from my brain. I think "step forward" as I move my left leg but then go sideways as though only my abductor muscles got the cue to move and I fall to the floor. I crawl spastically to the end of the bed and try to stand again. As I sway toward my dresser I put my arm out to catch myself but my wrist and elbow do not seem to realize they need to stiffen and I slam my chin and shoulder into the top drawer. I stumble wildly in this manner out of my bedroom and around the corner until I finally make it into the bathroom to the toilet.

For the next several hours I alternate between sitting up clumsily on the bed and stumbling around my bedroom trying to get my motor skills under control. I manage to let Tilda outside but cannot yet pick up the papers she dutifully made use of, bless her. Slowly, arduously, my mind clears from thick black to murky gray to hazy with occasional pockets of visibility. My right side persists in a state of extreme pain, but other bodily chaos gradually eases up save for occasional prolonged spasms in my face, neck and hands.

By late afternoon I am steady enough to move to the dining table. When I can sit in silent torture no longer I turn on my computer and in my e-mail inbox I find several new messages. I click on the top one first and before reading it I notice the date sent is March 25. I cannot make sense of the date; it might as well be Magly 57. I click over to my desktop calendar and see that March 25 is a Friday. I click back to e-mail and pull up the next message and see the same date. The lingering haze in my mind still will not let me comprehend what the date means. Clicking back over to the calendar I see that Friday, March 25 is highlighted in yellow, indicating it is today's date. I reach around the computer and pull the letter to my loved ones closer so I can see the date at the bottom. March 23. When the puzzle pieces finally lock into place I understand: I have been out for two days.

Only now does it occur to me that no one has called since I have been awake. Standing up gingerly I shuffle to the desk to get my phone and find five missed calls and three messages, the first being from Reese letting me know she could not make it to dinner Wednesday night. "Oh my God," I say out loud. A hammer of immense guilt slams down hard on my chest as I realize Tilda could have been left alone for an untold number of days. Then I think of what Reese would feel seeing me now, which is nothing compared to what she would have felt if she had been the one to find me dead. "Oh my God," I say again. Pressing my hand against the roaring pain in my side, the deluge of remorseful tears begins.

Chapter 6

It is Sunday, December 17, 2000. I am back on the leather-padded table with my eyes closed. Sue tells me to think retrospectively about my life. "Think now about who you were at age thirty," she says. "Think about where you were, what you were doing." I think back and recall I was in my third year of recovery from a spine-injuring auto accident. I was taking college classes while I could not work. I was just beginning a new relationship. "Now back to age twenty," Sue says. I see myself back in Dallas, dancing in clubs and working at a grocery store.

I follow Sue's instructions in this manner as she patiently continues. "Now back to age ten...then five...then two...and now you are back in the womb."

When she says, "And now you are back in the womb," I immediately feel frustrated. I feel extremely constricted and uncomfortable. I want to kick the walls down around me. I am aware of feeling aggressive because the space I am in is much too small and I need to break free.

Then Sue says, "And now you are at the point just before conception." Like a bolt of lightening I blast backwards through a tunnel of light and up into the cosmos far, far away. I travel on and on and on. When I finally stop I am suspended high up in the universe among the stars looking down upon Earth. As I float here peacefully without any form whatsoever, Sue asks me who I am and I reply with a voice so vast it is as though the cosmos itself is speaking: "I am The Message." I say I have waited a long, long time for just the right moment to come to this world. I watch my entry into Earth now; it is like a pinprick on the surface, tiny and entirely unnoticed by the masses. I watch as ripples of my impact begin to go out in concentric circles and eventually encircle the planet. I say, "I am to be revealed in this world as The Message."

After lingering here a few moments longer, Sue leads me to an entirely different place. It is a hallway filled with numerous doors on either side, and as I walk along I become aware of a door all the way at the end with white light gleaming all around it. This is the door I have been looking for. I run as fast as I can down the hall and as I reach for the handle a being of brilliantly luminous light opens the door, laughing. I know this being instantly and flush with ecstatic bliss and surprise, I love him so much. Behind him is a reception of several dozen supremely joyful, loving angels (light beings of different indistinct shapes), and I know and love all of them.

All the angels are laughing at me teasingly because it has taken me so long to find them. It is like I am late to my own party. "I'm sorry!" I say, laughing with them. "I didn't know how to get here!" They say they have been waiting for me so we could share important information. "We couldn't get started without you!"

After a lengthy period of walking through the crowd receiving warm greetings, we all move into a shimmering white room and sit in a U-shape with me at the base of the U. I am wearing a blue plaid flannel shirt as though to distinguish that I am the one who is to do the earthly work.

30

Shortly a majestic god-like being of bright white-gold light arrives and "sits" right in front of me. He puts his "hands" upon my shoulders and gently leans his "head" into mine. He waits a moment, then without speaking slowly gives me these words:

"This world [meaning the physical world] was not created as we think it was. We can see conflict throughout this world – throughout. This world was created through the conflicts of the people. You can see this. [And I could, more profoundly than I can convey.] We did not begin with conflicts as are seen in the Bible. Conflicts laid out in the Bible helped create and facilitate conflicts of our world. That is not how we started. We started with absolute love and peace. This is the point to which we must return."

There is a long pause to allow me to take all this in. There are countless layers of information coming into my awareness, as though I can see the impact and nuance of every single intention and action in the world. I say, "It's all so simple," and am about to continue with, "and we have made it so hard," when he begins speaking again:

"All this time people have believed in the mandates of their religions. Nations have warred. Brother has killed brother. All this based on false truths. What people turned to to justify their anger they didn't know was wrong. They just did not know." There is another brief pause before he ends our meeting with, "True truth rather than false truth. Bring these words and the angels home with you.

I breathe deeply, pause, and slowly begin to stretch my

arms and legs as I exhale. I feel Sue's hand lightly on my shoulder and hear her say, "Well done, Mary. Just lay here and relax for a few minutes. That's a lot to take in." Once again I have been "gone" for more than three hours and now long for an eternal sleep, which in this moment feels like the only way I will ever be able to take in the enormity of these experiences.

Chapter 7

I have an appointment with Dr. Joe Mancini and I am so excited I arrive twenty minutes early. Last week in our consultation visit Dr. Mancini surprised me by saying he would like to work with me. He eagerly laid out a plan: over the course of eight weekly sessions he will put me under hypnosis, ask me questions and record my answers. The goal is to get more direction from, control over, and clarity about, my visions and insights. I cannot believe my good fortune in finding this man.

I did not tell Dr. Mancini about my recent suicide attempt during our first visit. He does not know that in the painful aftermath of that failed effort I have yielded completely to the mess I am in and have spent most of my time these past weeks just trying to be still. I have felt no pressure or expectation or worry, nor have I felt self-compassion or self-pity. I just let go, and in doing so I have lacked any familiar rhythm of thoughts. Every day I have stared out the window at spring brightening Mother Nature's attire and felt neither resonance nor resentment. I have let the tears and time flow without trying to manage either. Dr. Mancini knows none of this.

He also does not know that for the past eleven years I have tried desperately to reconcile the two worlds I have lived in. That fateful weekend with Sue had left a residue of euphoria that for nearly two weeks had me gazing in wonder at everything – my body, the sky, furniture, traffic, it did not matter. In ironic timing, that blissful state of awe ended shortly after Christmas when out of the blue an anvil of confusion came crashing down on my psyche and paralyzed my ability to make sense of anything. Gorgeous, luminous scenes from ethereal realms continued to unfold at unpredictable times and by comparison this earthly existence seemed unthinkably complicated… and yet it was the existence in which I had to live. I did not talk about any of this during the consultation visit.

I simply told Dr. Mancini that I had really struggled to make sense of what was happening. I did not tell him that Sue had serious health issues and was not available to me after our initial work, so in my travels I had searched all over the world for someone else to help me process the wealth of Divine information I held inside. I told him I had "seen a lot of people" trying to get help over the years, but did not explain that meant *dozens* of western and eastern practitioners, from traditional therapists and doctors to acupuncturists and shamans. I did not mention the thousands of dollars I spent watching "healers" become nervous or intimidated or skeptical or downright dismissive when I told my story. I said, "I have felt pretty lonely trying to figure this out," but what I meant was that I knew no one else like me and knew no one in the entire world who could relate to or guide me. I meant that I have gone about my life with my well-practiced cheerful façade, but for the past eleven years my real feelings were most often ineptitude and insanity.

These are things I might have told him, but we were busy talking about my visions and insights.

In retrospect, perhaps I should have explained to Dr. Mancini that all this time I have kept my extraordinary secret from friends and family because I could never entertain the idea of openly accepting myself as a mystic – that would be like accepting myself as not real. I could have mentioned that long before I worked up the courage to take today's leap of faith with him there was a time I had been content with my little condo, my close group of friends, a loving relationship and, after transitioning from clinical research to nonprofit services, I was fulfilled in my work directing AIDS programs in America and Africa.

But if I had told Dr. Mancini this then I would have had to expound on the story and revisit the still-raw painful reality that my "normal" world had started crumbling more than two years ago when the organization for which I worked spiraled out of control after a disastrous change in board leadership and eventually had to close its doors. That happened at the same time the national economy spiraled out of control and took with it countless job opportunities that previously would have been plentiful for someone of my education and experience. It also happened at the same time that my home situation spiraled out of control after the condo association entered into a lawsuit with the building developer over numerous violations and I could not sell or rent or afford the mortgage. And it took no time at all then for the mounting financial pressures to take down my last remaining semblance of normalcy: my relationship. Every single day for the past two years I searched frantically for familiar security and every single day it eluded me. And all the while the calling of a spiritual journey echoed louder and louder against my ever-emptier heart.

When Dr. Mancini had asked how I found him, I said something along the lines of, "I was looking for someone with experience in mystical phenomenology, and in my research it appears you have worked with this kind of thing before." It did not seem necessary to clarify that just weeks before today's leap of faith I fell over a cliff instead, but that in that fall the miracle of surviving ninety-seven pills taken with three glasses of wine had shown me that I have two commanding forces living within me which in simplest terms I understand as Ego and Love. And that Ego is no longer in charge. And that this understanding helped me muster the courage to come to him and try to find out just exactly who or what this Love inside me is. Instead I just said, "I am so thrilled you want to work with me!"

If only he knew that the hard-fought surrender to this newfound Love feels like exhaling air that has been trapped at the bottom of my lungs all my life. If only he knew. Then perhaps as I breathed in new possibilities I would have handled the miracle he was about to give me with far more grace.

Chapter 8

I go places on my own now, most often unexpectedly. Today I am unexpectedly where I began, and here there is total darkness.

Suspended at its edge I gaze into this darkness, weightless and rapt. The emptiness of this darkness is an exquisite void unlike anything known on Earth. It is the purity of nothingness and the pure potential of everything, with no beginning and no end. Words cannot describe the infinite magnitude of this gorgeous darkness but it is appropriate to say it is the purest state of Love. It is also appropriate to call it God.

Into this God-Love moves a massive colorless "cloud" of vibration, which can best be described as infinitesimally small, empty, wave-like particles. These particles are latent energy. I experience this very clearly as being before there is BEing, or the potential for life before there is the living of life. I know this because I am one of these particles. As such, I am also in oneness with all surrounding particles, feeling the entire mass of vibration in unity but still aware of my singular self. I am simultaneously All and One.

There is an immediate symbiotic relationship between the potential of my latent energy and the pure potential of Love. Now Love can experience itself through my energy, and my energy can experience existence through Love's infinite potential. As Love's darkness fills every particle, including me, this "charges" our energy and we awaken to our first moment of conscious awareness.

Love's purity fills every particle but we cannot fill all of Love because it is infinite. There is and always will be more Love than energy, and therefore Love is both within and beyond all of life. Where Love exists, there is pure light, beyond that is always potential for pure light.

Every single speck of our energy has become a conscious particle of pure Love holding infinite potential and possibility, and every potential and possibility is equal. This Law of Equality is the fundamental law of the universe governing unconditional love: <u>All energy has potential, all potential is possible, and all potential and possibility are equal.</u>

Love is everything in potential form, including thought and perception. All Love-filled particles, now having awakened to conscious awareness, can bring the potential of thought and perception to life as a primary force of creation. Our thoughts will transform perceptions of energy from one form into another.

With crystal clarity I am aware of the instant I, as a particle of Love, become aware of myself as pure joyful energy and want to experience BEing who I Am. With my first thought I rocket myself with tremendous force into the beginning of my evolution. My thought is: I am goodness, and I want to BE all that I Am! As a single particle of collective Love consciousness, my longing to experience my own goodness is also Love's longing to experience its own goodness.   I become life experiencing God and God experiencing life.

Chapter 9

I notice that Dr. Mancini is not as chipper when he opens the door for our second visit. He is wearing a short-sleeved blue shirt, blue jeans and sandals, and rubs his gray beard nervously as he invites me in. He does not hold my gaze as I say hello but through his glasses I catch a hint of puffiness under his eyes that suggests he is not well rested.

Before I am even settled into the large brown recliner opposite the office chair in which Dr. Mancini seats himself he says, "Well, I'm afraid you're not going to want to hear what I have to tell you, Mary." As he speaks he tilts his head slightly down and forward as though he's trying to tell me the bad news telepathically.

I feel the blood drain from my face. "Oh?" I place my hands on the arms of the chair as if bracing to receive a blow. "But you're going to tell me anyway, aren't you?"

He holds up a file. "I went over the intake form you sent me after you left here last week. Don't you think it would have been important to tell me about your suicide attempt when you were here?"

I take a moment to consider the question. "Actually, no," I reply truthfully. "I came to you seeking help with my visions and insights, not my suicidal ideation."

He tilts his head to the side and purses his lips in condescension. "You can't seriously think a recent suicide attempt would not be important for me to know, *Mary*."

His patronizing tone catches me off guard. Without taking a moment to compassionately consider things from his perspective, I jump on the defensive. "Well, yes I can, *Joe*. Because we were focused on my metaphysical issues when I was here, not my emotional issues. You did not ask any questions about my emotional well being. Not one. You were eagerly focused on my mystical abilities because *that's* what I came to you for."

Realizing my point, he softens. "You're right, I did not ask those questions and I should have." He holds up the file again. "Normally I have clients complete their intake form before the consultation visit and for whatever reason I didn't do it that way this time, and I'm sorry. But the fact remains the work we planned would affect you emotionally. We have no idea what can come up in this kind of stuff, and given that I really don't think either of us are ready for this."

"You've got to be kidding." The inside of my head begins to hum loudly in disbelief. "I sent that form back to you the very day you e-mailed it to me. You had plenty of time to call me or e-mail me to talk about any concerns. Why did you let me go all this time believing we were going to start working together today?"

"I wanted to tell you in person because I didn't know how you would handle the disappointment." He shifts nervously in his seat and I can tell he is wishing he had handled this situation differently. "Look, I'm a hypnotherapist, not a counselor. After thinking this through I just don't feel qualified to handle such intense work with you yet given everything you've been through. I think it would be better for you to see a psychotherapist first."

My ears flush hotly at his last words. I say, very slowly, "Joe...I have tried... countless times... diligently and earnestly... to get help through psychotherapy." He stares at me in silence as I speak, his eyes narrowed as though to deflect any impact of my words. The bitterness of my pain wells up in a flash.

"You know, you have no fucking idea how hard I've tried to find someone to help hold me up through all of this." I cannot hold back. A familiar sense of beaten-down defeat floods my body and my speech becomes sloppy as I simultaneously talk and cry. "I have tried every way possible to get help with both my mystical abilities and the impact of having these abilities, and no one can help me. This lack of ability to get help – like what is happening again right this very minute – was a major contributor to my suicide attempt in the first place. Now you're just pushing me right back into that hell."

He gets up from his chair and walks toward me. "Mary, I'm *very* sorry for getting your hopes up." He opens his arms like he wants to hug me but my glare makes him stop. Instead he shuffles to the side and takes a piece of paper from the file he's holding. He says, "Look, here are the names of three therapists I can recommend who I know are likely to be receptive to complicated issues like yours. Just give one of these a chance and let's see what happens."

I take the paper from his hand and stand up to leave, shaking as I walk to the door. I turn around and say, "Thanks for nothing," as I wad the piece of paper up in my fist and close the door behind me.

I sit in my car outside Dr. Mancini's office with my head upon the steering wheel crying uncontrollably. I have no idea where to go. I have no idea what to do. I cannot fathom – not even for a moment – where the strength is going to come from to keep going. Once again I tried earnestly to get help, and once again I flatly failed.

I lean forward and scream into the windshield, "GODDAMN IT! GOD! DAMN! IT! GOD, DAMN IT! HELP ME!" I repeat the last part several times, pounding the steering wheel in rhythm with every DAMN IT I scream. When the thought occurs to me that this may be the moment I go completely mad I stop with one final slap of the steering wheel, defeated.

I fall back against the seat and look out the driver's side window at a row of trees beside a small ravine. I am emotionally exhausted to the marrow; I have been crying the same tears for far too many years. I stare at the trees and bite the end of my left thumb for several minutes trying to pull myself together enough to drive. I turn and numbly look around at the variety of custom brick homes in the neighborhood. Across the street to my right I watch a woman wearing a pink jogging suit walking her Jack Russell Terrier. I wonder where she came from and if she saw my outburst. When she passes beyond my view I catch sight of the piece of paper with the names of the three therapists on it lying on the passenger's seat, wadded up. I hesitate, sigh heavily with an exaggerated "pffffffff" and say, "Fuck you Joe Mancini." Then pick up the paper.

Without thinking about what I am going to say I dial the first number listed. No answer.

The name beside the next number is Margery Silverton. As I dial the number there is nothing in this moment – no rustle of wind through the trees, no ringing in my ears, no bolt of lightning – that gives away any hint that I am calling the miracle that will change the course of my life forevermore.

Chapter 10

My neighbor turns off his lawn mower and I close my eyes just to listen to the quiet for a moment. The instant my eyes close I am cradled in God's embrace. I feel him all around, holding me. I feel his intention to let me know there is safety in the truth of my spirit and All That Is.

As God holds me I become rich, burning gold. I am in the expansive blackness of the Love universe sitting on a large ornate chair that has a tall, wide back like a throne. I place my hands on the arms of the chair and look around.

I am taking in the blackness that is enveloping me when I become aware of light below me. I peer down through a floor that looks hazy as though it is some kind of veil and see numerous beings of light busily passing to and fro. The area appears to be a transit station of some sort. I am aware that these beings of light are able to be there and do their work because of the safety and security of the Divine space I occupy right now, and because of my presence in said space.

While watching this activity, something catches my eye to my left. I look over and see a formless God smirking at me in an ornery, teasing kind of way. I laugh out loud with shock. He is showing me there is fun here as well as seriousness. Without words I hear Him say in a playful gotcha! sort of tone, "You weren't expecting that now were you?" His love and adoration for me is so unfathomably pure I burst into tears.

Chapter 11

I have no expectations of success with Margery Silverton. I am resigned: she will either help me or she will not. I know better than to get my hopes up.

She immediately comes across as pragmatic and no nonsense, greeting me at the door of her office with a cautious though not disingenuous smile. "Come in and take a seat," she says, skipping pleasantries about weather or traffic to get right down to business.

Her dark wavy hair is in a short sensible cut. Her clothes are nice but not distracting – comfortable pants, comfortable blouse, comfortable sweater. Her office is small and functionally outfitted without feeling cramped or fussy. I sit on a blue plaid couch directly across from her and watch her move gracefully but deliberately as she writes something on a notepad on her desk and looks briefly for something among a small stack of papers. After a moment she raises her head to look me square in the eyes. "Okay, jump in wherever you want to," she says. "Whatever you feel is most important, start there."

Taking a deep breath, I start off with, "Oh man. There's so much convoluted shit to talk about I honestly don't even know where to begin." I glance around nervously and decide to talk first about my losses, but before I can get the first few sentences out I can tell by my tone and the pressure I feel pushing against my chest that I sound angry and defensive. I say, "I'm sorry, I think I'm going to sound mad at *you* as I rehash all this and I'm not, I'm just seriously frustrated."

Margery adeptly keeps the ball entirely in my court, offering neither sympathy nor a diversion from the issues. Leaning slightly forward in her chair she says, "I'm sure we're both aware that none of this is about me." She props her left elbow on her knee then and drapes her left forefinger over her lips, continuing to listen without giving away any hint as to what she's thinking.

When I finally speak about my visions and insights I am again defensive and through my bitterness I speak flippantly about other therapists not being able to help me. I say, "I usually end up feeling either like I'm babysitting them because they get nervous or intimidated, or that I've totally wasted my money because they don't believe me or they're incompetent. Mostly the latter." Still without any discernible expression Margery gives me some much needed perspective. "Mysticism isn't exactly something most of us get trained in handling, is it? I believe you know that firsthand." I cannot tell if by the end of our appointment she is going to kick me the curb or kick me in line.

The only notable reaction I see from her is when I talk about my suicide attempt and mention that I have not been to a doctor since I woke up and that the pain in my right side remains extreme at times. She raises her eyebrows in surprise.

After forty-five minutes of what feels like nonstop drama and self-pity coming out of my mouth, I worry that Margery thinks I have been overstating my situation just for attention. When I see her glance at the clock on the table beside the couch I hasten to let her know that even though I am a mess I am still very willing to work through all my issues and get to a better place. "I have surrendered to whatever is supposed to happen," I say earnestly. "I have tried everything and have no idea what to do now, no idea how to go about my life. I can – and *will* – do the work but I just can't be the project manager for myself right now. I need help."

When Margery speaks it is with such certitude there is little doubt in my mind that she can see through manipulative bullshit. So when the end of the appointment is at hand I desperately hope she understands and believes the truths I have just lain bare. I breathe in shallow, staccato breaths as she reveals her take on things. "It is entirely understandable that you are angry and depressed, Mary, you've suffered a lot of loss," she begins. "And it's also entirely understandable that you are confused; you have something literally out of this world that you have no choice but to face. I will be honest, you are certainly an unusual case and I don't have much experience working with someone like you. But I am willing to try if you are."

Whew. "I most certainly am, Margery. I really am. Thank you."

From that day on our work together progresses in a swift blur. I trust Margery completely, and she does not disappoint. Week after week she carefully holds every bit of my story as it unfolds and in the process manages to steady me emotionally and psychologically. In her office we proceed with classic talk therapy to deal with the losses and depression, and between visits she searches relentlessly for resources for both of us to have the support we need to do our respective work regarding the mystical events. She contacts colleagues and authors and researchers. She shares with me articles and interesting tidbits she found on mysticism, how the brain works, and the emerging field of neurotheology. She is Jewish but surprisingly knowledgeable about a wide range of religions, including Buddhism and Hinduism, and tells me about various practices or principles that may be of interest to me.

When at some point I ask Margery why she believed in me, why from the first day we met she thought my visions and insights could be real and not the result of a disturbed mind, she replied, "For several reasons. First, I was really struck by your sincerity in wanting to understand why all of these things were happening and by your determination to get better. But more than that, everything you said you 'see' in your insights was purely joyful. You spoke consistently about awareness, peace and transcendence, and from everything I've read in religious history, I know that is how true mystics speak. A disturbed mind, on the other hand is very fear-based. A delusional person doesn't talk like you do about love and bliss; they talk about fear. There was no fear whatsoever when you described your experiences."

As my work with Margery progresses I become aware that fear is a critical issue of exploration in my life – because I feel it decreasing significantly. I begin to feel noticeably lighter as the weight of embarrassment I have felt for so long in being different from everyone else gradually lifts. I do not think, "Today I am no longer going to be embarrassed because I don't like how it feels." Rather I begin to feel a powerful knowing rise up inside of me affirming that I cannot help who I am, nor will I hide it or suppress it any longer. In fact, I begin to fall gratefully in love with who I am because I have never known this me before. I begin to understand how to love myself *fearlessly, as I Am.* I make an effort to consider the miracle of surviving a suicide attempt that by every measure should have killed me, and the miracle of finding Margery within just weeks afterwards. And in these miracles I see without question that a force far greater than me will not let me fail; I *know* I have nothing whatsoever to fear.

When she feels I am psychologically stable enough to handle deeper work on my mystical abilities, Margery tells me it might be useful for me to see a man she trained with a few years ago named Dr. Rudy Bauer. He is a clinical psychologist who, along with his wife, runs the Washington Center for Consciousness Studies. He is well known in psychotherapy circles because he runs an accreditation program for mental healthcare providers certifying in phenomenology-related healing. In addition to his extensive training in Gestalt psychology, he has spent more than thirty years studying numerous eastern religious practices. Given all this, Margery believes my abilities will not faze Dr. Bauer in the least.

Chapter 12

I am relaxed in a chair when Archangel Michael appears to my left. He is gloriously handsome golden light. Even without form he appears strong beyond compare. He exudes deep wisdom and kindness.

Michael tells me my losses are important; that while it is hard, I do not "need" the things I think I have lost because I have other work to do. "It is good work," he says. "It is fulfilling work, but it is going to take time. That is where Love will be."

He says he knows I have been ready for this work, but everyone else around me wasn't ready. He laughs and says jokingly, "They're wimpy." There is such immense love for me in his laugh that I flush with warmth and comfort.

Michael tells me I have earned my robes, but I can see he means something other than robes, more like an apparel of light. As I am pondering this apparel of light I see "AWARENESS" arch over me, emanating from a large heavenly spotlight that is shining down upon me from behind.

"You are going to know things on a lot of levels," Michael says. "LOTS of different levels. Now it is going to get big." As he tells me this I feel myself backing into the heavenly spotlight behind me. It is as though I am backing away from Michael, but not in a bad way. He has work to do where he is needed and I have work to do where I am needed, which I understand now is where AWARENESS is rising.

Chapter 13

The Washington Center for Consciousness Studies is located in a handsome three-story row house near Dupont Circle. The warm sunlit front room where I wait nervously for my appointment is decorated with comfortable sofas and chairs and a mix of eastern and western art, photos and textiles. Surrounded by intricately patterned throw pillows, I sit on a sofa facing the window and pretend to read a copy of Shambhala Sun magazine while glancing around at the variety of cultural and religious imagery. A group of people just getting out of a seminar pass by on their way out, a few greet me with a silent bow or nod.

When I meet Dr. Bauer for my consultation I feel inexplicably awkward and fumble wildly with my thoughts. His third floor office is the size of a classroom and he is seated quite a distance from me in a simple wooden occasional chair in the middle of the room. As he asks me questions about my experiences I am distracted by his nice blue socks, which I can see clearly because he took off his shoes and now that he is barefoot he appears shorter even while sitting down. I wonder senselessly if he matched his expensive blue socks to his expensive blue shirt or the other way around. He is a few years older than me and his graying hair is longish and wavy. While he talks I wonder if the waves are natural, then I wonder why I am even wondering that, of course they are, how could they not be? Behind him are hundreds of books lining tall shelves and I wonder if in those books there are stories of people like me – and if so, has Dr. Bauer read them?

He tells me we should meet again; he is short on time now but can spend more time with me next week. Upon leaving I realize I have very little recollection of what I told him and remember very little of what he said to me. It was as though my brain had zoned out the entire time and I had drifted through the appointment on autopilot.

The second time I see Dr. Bauer I suspect it will be the last because I do not like the puzzling awkwardness I feel in his presence. But then another miracle happens.

Whatever I have been talking about he has evidently heard all he needs to know. He places the pen and the notebook in which he has been writing on the small table next to him and leans forward with his hands clasped casually together. He speaks softly and says, "Okay, let's just relax for a few minutes and see what happens here today."

He moves his chair a little closer to the couch where I am sitting and tells me to take a few deep breaths and let them out slowly, relaxing as much as I can on each exhale. As I am following his instructions he moves a little closer again and asks me to concentrate and see if I can feel his energy. I am thinking about how awkward this is when a warm energy lightly washes over me. "Close your eyes and tell me what you see," he says.

I close my eyes and see nothing but the jumble of light streaks and hazy darkness that one would expect to find in the back of their eyelids. "I don't see anything," I say flatly.

"That's perfectly fine," Dr. Bauer says, unfazed. "Just stay with it for a bit and let's just see if anything shows up."

I breathe and wait, breathe and wait for about a minute, then without any kind of transition the hazy nothingness I see turns into a crisp, vast blackness that I have seen before in my insights. Quickly I become like air filling this blackness. I am one with everything. I *am* everything. I tell Dr. Bauer what is happening and he speaks encouragingly, "This is good. In some theologies there is what is referred to as a stainless space, a place of pure nothingness. You're doing great, just stay focused and continue to tell me what you see."

While I am in/as this blackness, Jesus appears beside me to my left but his form is like a shell, empty. I immediately understand he has just returned to this place and I know what he needs. I "pour" my God-Oneness out through my hands and down through the top of his head into his body; as I do so my Oneness flows like gold-flecked light. When I have filled Jesus up entirely with my Oneness he becomes as I Am, embodied in the flesh.

The entire scene takes no more than twenty minutes to unfold, at which point Dr. Bauer says we have to stop.

At the end of the appointment, while Dr. Bauer is checking his schedule for the next available date to have me return, I ask him point blank: "So, am I crazy? Do others 'see' like I do?"

Dr. Bauer pauses, uncrosses his legs and closes the appointment book. He leans forward and says. "Not only are you not crazy, Mary, I'd say you have a profound gift of insight." Tears well up in my eyes as he continues. "I've been doing this a long time and I have seen countless clients. Most people spend their whole lives studying, training, meditating to go from A to B to C, step by step trying to get to the Z of spiritual wisdom. But you just jump from A to Z. The problem is that Z has no context for you because you skipped over all the usual steps that lead to such wisdom."

This is the moment. This is the aha! and ohhhh moment for which I have been waiting all these years. For the first time since my visions and insights began, I feel validated. It is no wonder I have felt crazy and alone: I started this journey at the destination point, and here evidently there aren't many fellow travelers. I want to rush over and squeeze Dr. Bauer with all my might, but instead I manage a teary, "Oh my God, I can't tell you how relieved I am to understand this. Thank you, thank you, thank you."

Before I leave his office Dr. Bauer encourages me to meditate daily, even if just for a few minutes, and he shares a few tips on what might work well for me since I know very little about the practice of quieting the mind. He is certain this will help me gain at least some measure of control over my visions and insights.

Armed with new understanding and tools, I leave feeling like a kite surfing the rays of the warm summer sun overhead. In the big scheme of life I have no idea what it means to have this profound ability, but as I walk to my car I make a firm commitment to wend my way along this mystical path and go wherever it takes me, be it on Earth or in heaven. It cannot be hell. I have already been there.

Chapter 14

During a brief morning meditation an image of the Mata Amma, India's Hindu "hugging saint," floats up in my mind's eye. I see her sweet smile, acknowledge her with a smile in return, and let the image float away.

Shortly an image of His Holiness the 14ᵗʰ Dalai Lama arises. I look at it only briefly, but that it is enough. I immediately feel a swift pull into the Dalai Lama's mind. As soon as I am firmly there I feel another swift pull through him, out of him, and into the 13ᵗʰ Dalai Lama's mind. Then the 12ᵗʰ Dalai Lama, then the 11ᵗʰ Dalai Lama. Each time it feels like a "plop!" into and out of each mind. I continue on like this all the way through the line of Dalai Lamas, and when I reach the 1ˢᵗ I feel a powerful leap out of his mind and into the mind of Buddha. I am here at the first moment he experiences enlightenment under the pipal tree.

I see all that Buddha sees in the expanse of All That Is. I become all the possibilities of existence and nothingness at once. I look at All That Is and I am All That Is. I watch the interplay between all energies, notice the snags and entanglements, and I see how the consciousness of emotions flows and alters directions and stagnates. I embody all of this. It feels like bobbing in an ocean of everything without touching anything. It is all and only absolute love and peace and equanimity that is at times falsely warped in perception by the snags and entanglements. I stay here with Buddha a while fascinated, absorbed, soaking it all in. We are not interpreting or assigning words to any part of the experience, we are just observing and understanding.

The moment I have the thought that I understand everything entirely, Buddha himself pops up in front of me and looks directly at me. He has no form, but it is clearly him. He is expansive, as though taking up much of the cosmos. He smiles with a playful, piercing joy that makes me immediately cry in ecstatic happiness. Without using words he says, "See? It's fun!"

Chapter 15

Margery Silverton, Dr. Bauer and I are on a mission. Collectively we have decided I need a supportive place in which to immerse myself in focused spiritual practice. It needs to be a place where I can have the solitude to cultivate my mystical abilities and yet have community in which to process what I know with the help of teachers and like-minded individuals who have words and ways to speak about Divine wisdom that thus far I do not have.

We make calls. We write letters. We search the internet. We explore options ranging from Christian convents to Hindu ashrams to Buddhist teaching centers. Dr. Bauer refers me to his contacts in New York, Arizona, Louisiana and California. He recommends Christian ministers I might want to meet, he makes sure I meet India's Mata Amma when she is in town, and he suggests I attend an eleven-day Buddhist teaching to be given in DC by His Holiness the Dalai Lama.

All these leads yield nothing until the week before the Dalai Lama arrives in Washington and I begin seeing the Dalai Lama and Buddha for the first time in my meditations. The morning I plan to go online to register for the Dalai Lama's teaching I spend twenty minutes in meditation as a spectacularly intricate, colorful circle swirling around Earth. I realize minutes later when I register for the teaching that the circle is the exact sand mandala shown on the registration website. While attending the teaching, in the presence of the Dalai Lama I feel a line of fire raging between my stomach, heart and throat.

The day the training ends I share all of this with Dr. Bauer, who happens to be on the host committee for the Dalai Lama's visit. He says, "I have a hunch you need to speak with a woman I sat next to at the teaching; we happened to exchange phone numbers. I think you should call her while she is still in the States. I just have a feeling."

The woman's name is Rinchen. She is part of the contingent traveling on tour with His Holiness the 17th Karmapa, the man presumed by many to take over as spiritual leader of Tibetan Buddhism when the Dalai Lama passes on. Dr. Bauer gives me Rinchen's phone number and says, "Just tell her your story and see what she says. Don't ask for anything, and don't expect anything, just tell her your story and let's see what happens."

I reach Rinchen as she is waiting to board a flight for New York, the next stop on the Dalai's Lama's U.S. tour. She is sitting in a noisy restaurant across from her gate and sounds irritable as she tries to hear me.

"I was given your number by Dr. Rudy Bauer, whom I think you met at the Dalai's Lama's teaching this week," I say loudly.

"Who?" she asks gruffly. I repeat myself. "Ohhh. Yes, Rudy Bauer, I know who you mean."

Feeling slightly unwelcomed, I start awkwardly with, "Dr. Bauer thought it might be good for me to introduce myself and tell you about some unusual experiences I have been having. I do not know why he wanted me to tell you, but if you don't mind..."

"Alright, go ahead," she says before I can finish my sentence.

I tell her as succinctly as I can about the kind of visions and insights I have been having for years and then tell her what began to happen around the Dalai Lama's visit to DC. She asks a few questions to make sure she understands, and then says, "Hang on, let me think for a minute."

I hear her say, "Thank you" to someone in the restaurant and then I hear shuffling of chairs. She says, "Hmmm," to herself but nothing more for a bit. Finally she says, "Okay, well, I think you should come to India. I can arrange a room for you near His Holiness's temple, no problem. When you get there I will make sure you get in to meet the Karmapa and you can tell him what you know and see what he says."

I am momentarily stunned silent.

"Wow," I finally manage. "I, uh, I will definitely think about it, thank you for such a generous offer."

"Look, I have to catch my flight now but e-mail me and we can work out particulars over the next few weeks while we're touring if you decide you want to do it." She gives me her e-mail address and says she will be in touch as she is able.

I have been pacing round and round along the edges of my living room rug during the conversation and now stop and put the phone down on the coffee table. I ease down onto the couch and say, "Holy shit," as I put my hands on my head and shake it back and forth. "Wow, wow, wow."

My mind is reeling with questions and shock. In all my international travels I have never for a moment considered going to India. Ironically, I have never considered it because I thought it might be too chaotic and spiritually woo-woo and I did not think I would be able to relate. In this moment now I realize this chaos and spiritual woo-woo-ness may be remarkably like my own mind.

Thirty minutes later I am still trying to process this unexpected possibility when Rinchen calls me back. Her flight was delayed briefly and she's been thinking more about our conversation.

"I just wanted to tell you I think you should consider coming to India for several months, even a year or longer if you can," she says. "In fact, get the visa that allows you to stay the longest. I think the Karmapa and others, including maybe even the Dalai Lama, may be interested in your experiences and it's possible they might work with you. I'm not promising anything, I'm just saying I think you should be open to all possibilities."

Chapter 16

I am part body, part spirit. My body is the front part of a massive cosmic spirit. I have a body because it is the part people can see, the thing that people can understand. It is what people can concretize and make sense of. But I am connected to this massive spirit, which is the consciousness of Christ. The consciousness of Christ and I are one and the same.

Behind me is a sky crammed full of white lights shaped like origami-styled doves. They are everywhere behind me but do not go beyond me.

Jesus is at the core of this Christ consciousness I/we occupy, so I inquire of him: Who are these beings behind me? Jesus tells me these are the souls I am to lead to a peace and happiness they have never known. These are the souls I am to lead to Christ.

.

Chapter 17

In the two months since my call with Rinchen I have sold or given away all my furniture. I sold my car. I gave away most of my clothes and household belongings. I turned the key to my condo over to the bank. And I placed precious Tilda in the care of my friend Nan, who lives across the street from the park in which Tilda and I have walked hundreds of times in the course of our five years together.

Most significantly, in this time I have finally managed to come out to my friends and family. I could not very well head off to live in India without explanation, so one by one I have had nervous dinners or phone calls with loved ones and put the truth out in the open: I am an unwitting mystic. I have not been able to go into great detail because I still do not know how to explain what happens to me or what I know, but I have at least managed to let them know the gist of what I have been keeping secret all these years.

To my great relief, across the board everyone has been amazingly supportive. They all affirmed their unconditional love and wanted to know why I had not told them sooner. No one pretended to understand but neither were they condescending or judgmental. The questions ran the gamut from curiosity to nonchalance. Reese asked, "Does what you 'see' foretell a better future for our world?" Mary, predictably, was all about the adventure: "So, not to push you along in your work and all, but how long do I have to wait before I can come visit and we can go to Nepal?" Nan had altogether different priorities: "Can

I use your golf clubs while you're off doing this spiritual thing?"

My traditionally-minded brother and sister were lovingly supportive, though they could not understand why I needed to go so far away and were suspicious of religious practices about which they were not familiar. My dear brother, without even pretending to disguise his skepticism, asked, "Now, you're not going to be sold into slavery or anything over there with this Dalai guy, are you? I looked him up and read something about him having slaves." I assured him that was likely a false rumor but would nonetheless take care to protect my personal freedom.

I did not have to come out to my mother; I have known very little of her since she divorced my father and left my brother, sister and me when we were young children. My father, however, has stayed in our lives and always been supportive of whatever we kids wanted to do, including moving halfway around the world. He has been ill for many years with myriad health problems so it is entirely possible he may pass away while I am abroad. I am conscious of this as we talk on the phone for what could be the last time, and because of this I am particularly struck by something he tells me that feels rather like a parting gift.

"You know," he says, delivering his classic sentence opener through a prolonged coughing fit, "if I had had the kind of courage you have now and been able to follow my heart, you kids would have grown up in Australia."

"What?" I have known the man for fifty years and never heard him say a word about this. "When did you want to go to Australia?"

"Oh, when you kids were young. I had all the paperwork filled out and had made the advance arrangements for a job through someone I knew, but then I just chickened out right at the last minute." He pauses for a moment, then says quietly, "You know, I chased a lot of dreams, but that was probably my biggest one and I just couldn't bring myself to ever go through with it. So I'm really proud of you for what you're doing, honey." He is crying now, and chokes out, "*Really* proud, don't you know."

"Ohhh, Dad. Thank you." I wipe my sleeve across my nose and cheek to catch my own tears. "That means the world to me. Don't you worry, I will take you to India with me in my heart so you can still have some of that adventure."

He blows his nose and gathers himself confidently. "Well alright, I guess I can go with you like that then. But don't eat too much of that spicy food or you'll give me heartburn." He laughs and coughs simultaneously at his own joke.

"Okay, I'll try to take it easy on you, Dad." I am relieved at the change in conversational tone. I do not want what will likely be our last phone call to end with the sadness inherent in unspoken finality. We manage to end the call gracefully with both of us saying, "I will always love you."

As I sit on the plane at Dulles airport awaiting departure, with my passport and a ten-year visa tucked into my backpack under the seat in front of me, I lean my head back and think about all the miracles that have unfolded in the short six months since my suicide attempt. Wow, how different my life feels in this moment. It is almost too much for me to believe. I cannot even imagine how life will feel in India.

I close my eyes and try to envision how things might unfold. The word "magical" begins to roam through my mind for the first of what will be many times.

Chapter 18

I am nodding off to sleep holding an image of Jesus in my mind because it feels soothing and familiar. Suddenly I see Jesus walk swiftly toward me, his heavy robe gathered up in one hand and a cup in the other hand. I become overwhelmed with an urgent desire to meditate.

I sit up straight and welcome the energy of Jesus into my body. Immediately I see an image I have seen many times in my meditations: a young man in a maroon robe meditating beside a small reflective pool of water, and another young man in a white robe behind him sitting upon a large rock also meditating. In previous visions, the young man by the water has had his back to me so I could not see him, and the young man on the rock was slightly turned away with his head tilted downward so I could not see him either.

Now both young men are turned so that I can see them, and I recognize them at once as young Buddha and young Jesus. As I recognize them, the two stand up and come together facing me. They present themselves and let me know they are both here to work with and guide me.

Later I awake from a light sleep seeing with crystal clarity that Buddha is identified with my mind, Jesus is identified with my heart, and "I" (as human) am identified with the core of my stomach. As I take this in, I feel the three of us begin to hum like an electric current in unison. I understand that Buddha will help me untangle and clear the jumbled mess of my mind and Jesus will help me open and purify my heart.

Part 2

You cannot travel the path until you become the path itself.

~Buddha

Chapter 19

Jesus and His Holiness the Dalai Lama are standing very close in front of me. In unison they both lean their heads in toward mine. I touch my forehead against each of their foreheads and feel overwhelming peace. We remain like this, the three of us touching heads and letting our light hold all of planet Earth in a state of peace.

Chapter 20

Despite what some people say, I believe India is, in fact, for the faint of heart. Here there is surely enough stimulation to jolt every sense to life, and enough unpredictability to teach even the meekest of spirits great fortitude.

The lengthy jaunts from airports to hotels to more airports and more hotels and eventually to my final destination provide my first schooling on life à la India:

1. This country is rich in many things, but efficient infrastructure is not one of them. Since this is not the fault of people trying to help me, when I look at the people and not the problems I am more likely to discover where some of the riches are hidden.

2. A '3-star' hotel rating is seriously relative.

   It may be located in what looks like a narrow alley. This narrow alley may be a real street in which two cars traveling in opposite directions, sometimes even in the same direction, can miraculously pass each other unscathed.

   A lock for the hotel room door may not automatically be part of the deal. Some smaller places give keys only upon request so they can keep track of them and do not have to keep replacing the ones tourists forget to return.

   What I receive from room service may not in any way resemble what I thought I ordered. People really seemed eager to give me what I wanted but could not understand my non-Indian English so they just gave me their best guess. Mistaken food tastes much better when I imagine there is kind intention that went into getting it to me.

I must keep on hand paper copies of everything related to hotel confirmations, including proof that someone was supposed to pick me at the airport and that airport pick up and drop off were included in the price. Many hotels do not have internet service onsite or may not have it at the time of arrival, so any reservation information I provide is helpful for all involved.

3. Airport adventures in India are one great big lesson in patience.

Just because the flight I chose to Dharamsala has a daily departure time of 11:15 does not mean it actually goes out every day. It just means that IF the flight goes out that day it might go at that time or it might go at some other time. Flights to smaller destinations often do not depart until the day they have enough passengers to make the trip worth the cost. Flights to mountainous regions are also subject to frequent delays and cancellations due to storms and fog.

Just because the person in front of me gets hotel compensation for a canceled flight does not mean I am going to get it. In fact, I should not assume I will receive the same information, ticket or treatment as the person in front of me at any time. The situation may look the same to me, but apparently it may look quite different to the person to whom I am speaking. I am best off being kind so as not to make the situation worse, patient so as not to appear entitled, and mindful so as to invoke the power of peace inherent in the Buddhist teachings of non-reaction.

4. It may be wrong to assume that my room at a guesthouse comes with toilet paper. Or bedding. Or towels or soap. Or appliances or dishes or running water in the "kitchen." The opportunity to learn how to navigate local shops, however, is complimentary.

My first residence in this frenetic country is a sparse, profusely pink room on the second floor of a white guesthouse in the dusty village of Sidhbari. My furnishings when I arrive are a frameless twin bed, a small wooden end table and a white plastic chair. The morning after my arrival the landlady kindly walks me to a neighboring village to show me the local commercial scene. From several ramshackle shops I add to my furnishings new bedding, a small bookshelf, a stainless steel bowl, a spoon and a cup with red hearts all over it. To balance out the space with an appropriately austere spiritual tone I hang a cheap string of Tibetan prayer flags in a half circle under the light switch and slip the knotted end of a souvenir-grade brocade panel with auspicious Buddhist symbols on it over a nail already in place beside the bathroom.

Sidhbari sits at the foothills of the Himalaya Mountains in northern India, just east of Pakistan and just west over the jagged Dauladar mountain range from China. It is primarily a single-street line of houses and shack shops that evolved in makeshift fashion along a busy trade road, just as most other small towns and villages did throughout all of India, according to a local taxi driver. Its claim to fame is His Holiness the Dalai Lama's picturesque Gyuto Monastery, which is nestled in a dramatic setting against the mountains, and which currently serves as the temporary residence of the exiled and highly revered Buddhist lama His Holiness the 17th Karmapa.

As I imagine is true of all of India, Sidhbari is proudly colorful. Women everywhere, even those working in the terraced rice fields surrounding the village, wear traditional salwaar kameez (long blouse with pants) and flowing chunnis (scarves) of luscious colors that seem to linger for a moment in the space just behind where the women walk. The ubiquitous Buddhist monks and nuns wear flowing maroon and saffron robes, unless they are Korean, in which case they sometimes wear roomy gray Asian-style shirts and pants. The gentle faces of Sikh men are accented above with colorful tightly wound turbans and below with bulging black or gray beards. Tibetan prayer flags flutter their green, blue, yellow, red and white mantras from tree limbs, banisters and rooftops. Indian shopkeepers and drivers drape strings of plastic marigolds and other bright flowers along windows, dashboards and roofs. Everywhere I look my eyes find sights in which to delight.

For my ears, there is also more than enough stimulation. Like other small villages I was driven through to get here, Sidhbari is incredibly noisy. The noise comes foremost from the crumbing, barely two-lane road upon which most buildings sit. Everything and everyone share this road. Every manner of vehicle and motorbike pass along using their horns incessantly to communicate with each other, pedestrians, animals and friends. Herds of chattering animals and school children are shepherded through. Whistling neighbors and barking dogs trot back and forth. Military tanks and over-crowded town buses rumble past and over-worked brakes squeal constantly in anguish. In the evening when the traffic begins to calm, the bar across the street, which also sells firecrackers and bigger things that go BOOM, picks up where the mobile life leaves off.

From morning to night Sidhbari is a ceaseless cacophony of noise.

The air in Sidhbari is also chock-full of activity. The inviting aromas include the exotic spiciness of curry and cardamom wafting from kitchen windows around midday and early evening, and occasionally a floral-sugary scent I have yet to identify dawdles outside my window in the morning. The uninviting aromas include the sharp sting of exhaust fumes, the suffocating swell of smoke from burning trash and the pungent sweaty odor of animal hide.

All around me is evidence I am a far cry from the westernized land of plenty. This is more the land of make do, with heavy reliance on old-fashioned ways. Squatted in small courtyards and on the banks of streams, women beat clothes clean with stones and makeshift wooden paddles, then hang them to dry over railings and bushes and barns. Most homes do not have air conditioning or heat and electricity is not always available, so dotting the front of most houses are porch sitters making use of the natural airflow and light to wash vegetables, help children with homework or just take a moment to pause with family and friends.

There are not nearly enough jobs in this area the keep the masses employed, so in shops and offices or just randomly on the sides of the streets I see groups of men doing tasks that could be done by one person or by machine. Government and business processes also appear to be intentionally inefficient (bafflingly so in some cases) so as to give more people an opportunity to participate. In the large agrarian community, however, there is plenty for everyone in the farmer's family to do. It is not uncommon to see women doing hard labor tasks such as digging ditches and wielding large farm tools (always in their colorful salwaar kameez) and to see men and women both transporting incredibly heavy loads of everything from crop yields to full buckets of rocks on their heads.

Amid all this frenzy there is one daily pastime in which virtually every adult engages that makes everything seem manageable: they stop to have chai. Several times a day in business offices, shops and homes everywhere someone is making, serving or having black tea boiled with milk, fresh ginger, cardamom, cinnamon, water and sugar. It is served piping hot, often in small glasses so hot one has to hold from the top and drink slowly. It is a charmingly simple way to step back from the liveliness of days here.

As I settle in to this fascinating country to explore my spiritual path free from worldly concerns, it is apparent India is going to teach me things in a way that only India can. Whatever lessons lie around the dusty corner I will try my best to meet them head on with gratitude and, if I am lucky, grace. And on the days when the grace seems a little too hard to come by I will try to remember just to relax, have a glass of chai, and momentarily leave unattended the commotion of India and my own mind.

Chapter 21

I am "inside" the Christ consciousness talking with Jesus about his death. Why did he not leave town before he was killed? Was his crucifixion preordained... (he shakes his head no)... or was it a decision he made on his own?

"It wasn't a decision as much as an acceptance," Jesus says. "It would have happened anyway. Because of the circumstances [of that time] it could have happened at many times in many ways in many places. So, first of all, it didn't matter that it was then. But also...the time was right for all involved, not just me.

"...There would have been more people hurt, more people who suffered unnecessarily had it happened any other time. So, in that moment, the number of people who were guilty, and I don't use that word in a bad way, but the number of people who brought about [my death], was much more minimal. It would have been much broader spread had it waited. Even in the way and the time that it happened, far too many people suffered because of it. But far less suffered because of the time that it happened than would have later, by the thousands."

Chapter 22

In this area of India many people are fond of saying, "Slowly, slowly." It is true, expectations do seem to soften if one adopts a longer-term view of things here. But then again, sometimes things can come about very quickly.

Just five days after I arrive in Sidhbari, before my mind and body have caught up with the nine and a half-hour time difference from the states, I find myself in a much-sooner-than-expected private audience with His Holiness the 17th Karmapa.

In Tibetan Buddhism, the Karmapa ("embodiment of Buddha's activities") is said to be the oldest continuously reincarnated spiritual teacher. He is a lama who reportedly nine hundred and one years ago decided to keep coming back to help others until suffering in all beings ceases. In 1992 a seven-year-old Tibetan boy known by the community to be "special" at birth, instructed his family to move to a specific area where a group of Tibetan monks would find him when they came searching for him. Those monks did indeed come and soon identified him as the 17th incarnation of the Karmapa. In late 1999, the then fourteen-year-old Karmapa pretended to go into isolated retreat but instead changed out of his robes and into civilian clothes and was secreted out of Tibet through Nepal and into India by car, foot, horseback, helicopter, train and taxi, and has been living in exile here ever since.

Today His Holiness is a tall, handsome young man known to be especially kind and intelligent. I meet him in a large room in the Dalai Lama's Gyuto monastery, where he currently resides. The room is lighted only by a row of windows that face out toward the hill upon which the monastery sits. Among the stately Tibetan tapestries and pictures of His Holiness the 14th Dalai Lama are four assistants and security officers standing with their hands clasped patiently in front of them.

I am not prepared for this meeting. I have not gained enough mental clarity yet to think about how to tell this important man about my visions and insights, nor have I thought about what I might ask of him, if anything. I do not know how the meeting came about so quickly; I just showed up at the appointed time as instructed by Rinchen. After a brief interview with a sharply dressed man in a black suit who appears to be the chief of security, here I am rambling to a radiant young Tibetan man who speaks little English. The ironic first words from the gently spoken nine-hundred-and-one-year-old lama are: "Slowly, slowly."

I tell him as succinctly as I can about my experiences, particularly as they relate to Buddha and the Dalai Lama. As I speak I see his eyes roll up and back slightly in his head, like he is listening to me with his ears and taking in information on another level at the same time. He asks questions about my work, my life, where I live and if I have studied Buddhist doctrine.

When he has heard all he needs to know he again rolls his eyes up and slightly back, this time taking a moment before he speaks, as though he is bringing words forth from a different place. His tone now is paternal. "First, you must learn who YOU really are," he says in halted English. As he says "YOU" he reaches up and gestures in circular brushing motions with his hands close to the sides of my head. "Slowly, slowly. You must learn this fully."

This is a laser sharp bull's-eye hit to my psyche. The question of who I really am has been a source of extreme confusion ever since my metaphysical experiences began. In my visions and insights I "am" pure white light, pure peace, pure Truth, The Message, Oneness, and so on. I have "been" the body of Christ and the mind of Buddha. My "higher self" is everything in the universe at once.

Given this confusion, before coming to India I made a firm decision to see myself simply as a compassionate human being with a profound ability to connect with Divine truth, period. This would allow me to approach this spiritual journey with the least confusion, and let me focus instead on how my abilities may benefit others. So what the Karmapa is telling me to do now I do not want to do.

But I am not about to disrespect a high lama by debating or second-guessing him. After a few more minutes of conversation I thank His Holiness humbly for his time and, feeling a bit deflated, prepare to leave. He laughs lightly, seeing that I was hoping for something other than the guidance he gave me. He tilts his head to look me in the eyes as he bows slightly and says, "Please return to keep me updated and to ask more questions as you need. When you are ready. When YOU are ready."

I walk back to my room letting the idea of "slowly, slowly" sink in because that feels easier than focusing on the directive to learn who I really am. Slowly, slowly feels so easy in fact it becomes the focus of my meditations and the subject of prayers almost obsessively every day for the next two weeks. As I keep this focus I begin to feel a deep trust developing inside me and know without question that my direction will be made clear when the time is right.

That right time comes on a noisy morning during a restless meditation when, as though a bing! sound pops up in my mind, it suddenly becomes clear to me that the Karmapa did not mean for me to learn who I am in terms of a label. He meant for me to understand what I know. He knew from our conversation that I had not had an opportunity to explore my abilities or to reflect on my knowledge in any prolonged, focused or studied manner. I realize now this was why he had instructed me to slowly and fully learn "who I really am" while gesturing around my head.

I cannot sit still with this realization in my already restless meditation and with the incessant noise continuing all around me, so I get up to go for a walk and think about things more informally. When I open the gate leading out to the street, my taxi driver friend, Yogesh, is directly in front of me leaning against his car. Without thinking, I say, "Yogesh, do you know of a really quiet place I could live around here? He thinks for a moment, then says, "I know a place. You should talk to them."

After a ten-minute drive up steep hills and a ten-minute walk through terraced rice fields, I arrive at my new home.

Thosamling (Tibetan for "place of study and reflection") is the first nunnery and institute for international Buddhist nuns and lay practitioners supportive of Buddhist practices in India. It is a small, isolated community of women from all over the world who live in silent resident rooms and share meals together in a common dining hall. In addition to an on-site teacher, temple and library, residents can attend Buddhist teachings by four major teachers in this area, including His Holiness the Dalai Lama and His Holiness the Karmapa. If guests do not wish to attend teachings they can also stay in silent retreat in their rooms. The goal is simply to support the spiritual work of each woman with the expectation that ultimately all work towards peace benefits all beings.

My inviting little corner room is bright white, with a large three-panel window that looks out onto wild flowers, terraced fields and the mountains. The sun rises over the far edge of range and streams directly onto my bed. Unlike Sidhbari, this is a blessedly peaceful, quiet home.

I came to India to talk with spiritual leaders, immerse myself in an intensive learning environment and find a supportive community that can foster and support me as I explore my Divine knowledge. Now that I have found that community, my work begins in earnest. I do not have a road map and I have no idea what I am doing or where I am heading; I will just have to take each day as it comes. When the time is right I will meet other spiritual leaders and will return to speak with His Holiness the Karmapa, but in the meantime I have been given an incredible opportunity now to study, reflect, meditate deeply and talk with others in a supportive spiritual learning environment. It is truly more than I could have hoped for. Today my slowly, slowly is right here, right now. Understanding this, the serene peace I feel causes me to question if perhaps right here, right now is in actuality all I really am and all I can ever really know.

Chapter 23

For three successive nights my dreams are filled with fear. I cannot remember the details after I awaken but vividly remember feeling like fears of all kinds were processing through me as though my body was a sieve. During meditation fear creeps into my mind through vague hints of random insecurities and worries, as if testing me to see if I will take the bait. I have a powerful desire to sleep during the day when I cannot focus on meditation and when I finally give in I have more fear dreams.

Shortly after I awaken on the third morning after these dreams begin I encounter Jesus and am told to go with him. He sweeps me up in his arms and we travel low above Earth first to Israel.

Here I am shown in minute detail the roots of the oldest, deepest fears in the hearts of the Jewish population and in the long-flowing mindstreams of government. The fear I see goes far, far beneath the current day façade of righteous political posturing and rigid theological or academic postulations. In simplest terms, I see that these old fears originated in sincerely well-intended concerns about breaking what was thought to be God's Laws. I understand that the details of those Laws are not relevant; the point of this lesson is to see that the fear that has driven this population for millennia was originally rooted in sincerely compassionate intention. I can actually feel that intention in the hearts of those who thousands of years ago first grasped this fear tightly and created the foundation for today's defensive, conflict-driven mindset. As I take this in

I feel enormous compassion emanating from Jesus and flowing through me.

Intertwined with this fear in the Jewish population, I also see in fine detail the nature of a relatively newer kind of fear the Palestinians face, which in simplest terms is driven by desperate fear of abandonment by God, Earth and Man. I feel the origins of this fear like a massive pleading to be held and understood and accepted.

Jesus and I next go to China. Here, again in great detail, I see what drives the government to control the masses in the way they do. Ironically, the foundation of the original motives is both compassionate and fear-based. I see there is an ancient, deeply engrained fear that the masses will lose hope if things do not appear orderly and safe, and if the masses lose hope then there is fear of chaos and large-scale loss of control.

Jesus now takes me to Russia, where yet a different kind of fear drives the government. Here I see is a much deeper self-serving fear seeded by rulers concerned for their own potential loss of power and privilege, which ironically resulted in a false sense of personal freedom for the masses. The energy of the population feels rugged; proudly and hardily toughened from the dynamics that literally govern their life.

The knowledge of these fears and the way people are driven/controlled/comforted by them is layered with countless nuances, like eddy currents and boulders in long rivers of fears that affect the flow and direction of life in numerous ways. In each country I experience the roots and impact of fear from the perspectives of both the governments and the people in totality as though I am living all minds and dynamics at once. In this way I see fear from the same universal perspective as Jesus sees it, compassionately understanding the original intentions and how the impact of these intentions eventually became entrenched mindsets of fear that rule nations and determine in extraordinary measure how the world operates. And I understand this is the same way fear came to rule the minds of individuals: it is the ultimate well intended but blindly perpetuated hand-me-down from and to every human being.

Chapter 24

Enlightenment is not for wimps.

I have just completed my first attempt at an isolated ten-day silent meditation retreat, and note the following lessons to ensure future retreats can be a) done in isolation; b) ten days long; c) silent and; d) meditative:

1. Do not attempt to start it on the day my previous month's lodging and food bill has finally been calculated. The earnest office assistant might forget I am in silent retreat and call me to the office to review her calculations because she wants to be fair. She might then say with an apologetic expression after glancing at my IN SILENCE badge, "Please can you pay as soon as possible?"

2. Do not attempt to re-enter a meditative state after lunch on the second day just as Mother Nature is putting up a full rainbow, end-to-end, right in front of me while snow is falling on the Himalayas in the background. I may not be able to resist grabbing my camera and running like a mad woman to capture the glory of the moment to remind myself of the magnitude of distraction dangers that abound.

3. Do not assume food poisoning will bring about any measure of enlightenment on days three, four or five.

4. Do not assume a meditative state is possible on the afternoon of day seven if, shortly after my retreat, I will be attending teachings with the Dalai Lama. I may be asked to complete security forms and provide copies of my passport and visa, then I may have to walk twenty minutes each way to/from the nearby village to get two passport photos. And upon finding out the photo shop's camera is broken I may have to walk thirty minutes each way to/from another nearby village again on day eight to complete my task.

5. Do not assume, while in the village on day eight and feeling that my retreat has been a total bust, that I can say to myself, "Damn it all, this is ridiculous! I admit

defeat! I am just going to go into this little garden restaurant, have a little snack, and even though it will be seriously frowned upon if anyone finds out, I'm going to have my first glass of wine in India!" As unlikely as it might be during the hours when everyone is usually studying, praying or meditating, before the waitress even gets to my table one of the Thosamling nuns might just wander into the garden restaurant to take some pictures of the lovely area with her new camera. And then she might join me to have a nice cup of tea as I enjoy a nice glass of freshly squeezed orange juice.

Chapter 25

I become aware of myself as Jesus standing on a hillside and looking outward. I realize the location is the Mount of Beatitudes.

To my right are people who had earlier gathered to listen to my talk. They are leaving and I know in this moment as I stand here that these people have not taken in my words to live for themselves. Instead, they have revered me for having said the words. In doing so, they will rely on me for their wisdom rather than fully understanding and embodying the wisdom for themselves.

In this way, I, Christ, have not become a part of them; I am set apart from them. I, Christ, was in the WORDS I spoke, but because of others' reverence for me and lack of belief in their own divinity they have not embodied me. Therefore I, Christ, cannot be known in the hearts of these people.

Chapter 26

It has been a long day. I have been sitting for hours atop a small mat squished up alongside others on a cold concrete floor in the English-speaking section of His Holiness the Dalai Lama's temple in the chilly mountaintop town of McLeod-ganj. It is the first of three days of teachings and thankfully this morning I was taken under the wings of three Korean nuns who showed me how to maneuver around the surprisingly aggressive crowd. I catch up with the nuns as we walk out of the temple and they lead me to the taxi we will share back to the footbridge near Thosamling. We all pile into an economy-sized car with a young Hindu Indian driver and begin winding our way down the mountain.

Shortly the nuns are talking about something in Korean and I hear one of them say the word "Christmas." So I ask if any of them are going to be in town for Christmas, since there is a big event out of town at that time and most nuns are planning to go. One of the nuns says she is not going and will be here that day, so I invite her to come to lunch with me and a few other women who are going to celebrate the holiday at a local restaurant.

I say to the nun, "I do hope you will join us. But I will tell you now you should be prepared, as there is going to be dancing. The Swedish woman who is organizing this little gathering is insisting we all do the chicken dance as part of the festivities. Of course, if you're more comfortable singing you can just do that."

The nun is quiet for a moment, then – seriously – breaks out in the most angelic voice singing the Christmas carol *Joy to the World*. And then the two other nuns join in. Then I join in and the taxi driver joins in. Three Korean Buddhist nuns, a twenty-something Hindu taxi driver and I are all crammed in a tiny car winding our way down a narrow mountain road, singing a song about baby Jesus. The entire song.

In this moment we are seriously putting out the message of joy to the world, loud and proud. And it is awesome.

Chapter 27

During meditation I feel slightly unsettling energy rise in something akin to warm waves rolling upward through the center of my body and splashing gently into my consciousness. The waves rise up in this order:

> *I <u>really</u> am no longer in the world in the way that was familiar to me for fifty years.*

> *I <u>really</u> have a whole new life.*

> *I don't know how to do this new life... no one can help me... I am alone.*

> *I still want aspects of my old life... I have important work to do... important work to do...*

> *Where am "I" in this new life of important work?... I still have dreams... this work is important... but "I" am important... important work... important...*

Just as all of this energetic angst reaches a gently panicked pitch, quite suddenly I get violently ill with projectile vomiting and diarrhea and stay sick for three days.

Now something is definitely different. When I go back into meditation not only is all my angst and questioning gone, waves of pristine clarity begin to joyfully ease into my consciousness:

> *My life is not old or new. It is <u>now</u>, always. I can literally SEE the expanse of <u>now</u> as though it is a*

world of its own.

I am doing this <u>now</u> beautifully, and all that was good from my past is still in me, helping me. I can literally FEEL my past, physically.

"I" and my important work are inseparable. I can bring my dreams and my mystical gifts along on the same path. I watch as numerous separated aspects of my "self" come together, then I feel myself become whole.

I am right where I should be now and can direct my path toward whatever beckons my heart peacefully at any time. <u>Now</u> becomes as big as the universe, with all concepts of time gone.

With a deeply calm feeling of internal integration, I close my eyes to sleep for the night and have rich, vivid dreams in which I travel above the stars to an enchanting sea of shimmering silk-like dunes where loving kindness is the only state of existence.

I awake feeling ready to meditate on the subject of perfect love and wisdom, for this is the place from which Jesus has shown me his healing words for the world will come. Jesus also told me I am to understand the journey to that place and help others understand the journey as well.

I take several hours to let concentrated points of vibrations very, very slowly seep down through every inch of the inside of my body, starting under the crown of my head and going all the way to the tips of my toes. It feels like a soothing internal massage. Once my whole body is in a steady vibrational state I achieve exquisite visionary openness. In the process of getting to this point I also experience numerous flashes of random, seemingly meaningless memories that have been stored up over my lifetime in various places in my body.

As I go through this slow process I also focus on perfect love as though it is an object, like a ball traveling through my body with the vibrations. Eventually, as though drifting in from thousands of miles away, the awareness of pure <u>forgiveness</u> *gently comes into my consciousness. In my deeply meditative state I do not hold onto to this awareness, I just acknowledge it and let it be. But then it comes back to me like a gentle command, as if to say, "No, look at it."*

I feel myself thickly, vaguely responding to the command with confidence that I have done well in forgiving in this lifetime; I am not holding onto to any unresolved hurt or anger as far as I know. Almost simultaneous to my thought of confidence, a long string of beads like one finds on malas or rosaries comes into my mind's eye. And every bead is a person. These are all the people from my adult life who have hurt me, upset me, or have been hurt or upset by me – many of whom I had not even known I had hurt or upset. Some of these people I knew only in passing and others I know well.

One by one each bead-person presents itself to me, and as they do I see all the ways that true, perfect loving forgiveness has not taken place. Most surprisingly, I can

111

see how I have not understood that I was the one who needed to be forgiven for my part in even the smallest minor annoyances – even if I had only hurt people <u>with my thoughts</u>. One by one, I methodically go through the string of people and take in the truth. I let go of any feeling except love, forgiving them and myself entirely and humbly asking for forgiveness of others wherever necessary.

Once the meditation is over it does not surprise me that pure forgiveness was part of my lesson while trying to learn about perfect love. When Jesus showed me that his words will come from a place of perfect love and wisdom he also showed me that he did not for one moment ponder the actions of those who brought about his death and then make a decision to forgive them: he never considered them "guilty" to begin with. There was nothing to forgive.

I am, however, surprised to find the wisdom of pure forgiveness revealed so meticulously and so lovingly within my own being. The lesson itself was purely forgiving, causing me no pain or guilt, just perfect understanding and acceptance. It opened my heart to a kind of peace I have never known, and I understand now in a much deeper way why forgiveness of others and ourselves is the most important act of love we can ever do. It is <u>the key</u> to healing old sorrows.

Chapter 28

Today I end a twenty-one day silent retreat. I fasted for the first seven days of this work in an effort to have as little interference as possible on my energy so I could explore in great detail all that exists between my current state of being and the state of being 100% pure love. This has been a tough retreat and I am relieved this day has finally arrived.

One reason this work has been particularly hard is because of a neighboring resident. Even though the building in which I live has a policy of silence and there are SILENT AREA signs all around, one of the fellow residents is a chatterbox who cannot keep silent to save her life. She appears to struggle with mild paranoia, so all day long she stops people in the echoing concrete corridors and goes on in conspiratorial tones about other residents. Not a single day has gone by in my retreat when her voice has not wafted into my awareness and distracted me. I am cognizant of the fact that this annoyance chronically invaded my awareness during an examination of pure love.

I made miraculous strides in this retreat and have gained valuable understanding and growth. After two weeks I was even able to see Chatterbox as a teacher and have been compassionately holding her in my heart with gratitude and love ever since.

I feel happily liberated now as I head to the dining hall for lunch. It is raining, so most residents are eating indoors instead of sitting in scattered places around the outdoor patios. Usually I find the indoor dining days awkward since we often eat in silence and sitting so close together makes me more self conscious of every noise. Today, however, I am happy to be around others.

The long dining table is full and the only available seat is directly across from Chatterbox. I take my seat, bow my head and say my blessing. When I finally look up and pick up my fork, my neighbor leans over and whispers a question to me about my availability for help with a task after lunch. I whisper back, "Sure, no problem."

Chatterbox drops her fork loudly on her plate and says in a nastily angry tone, "You know, the hardest part of my practice is silence, and I don't need *you* ruining my time to eat in peace. You may be free from your silence but some of us are still working on ours." She glares at me then with eyebrows raised, as if daring me to utter any sound in response.

Everyone in the room is stunned, and I am completely paralyzed. Days of blissful joy and compassion are instantly gone, replaced with the stabbing pain of embarrassment and humiliation. The very woman whose interference in my own peace of mind I have been using to deepen my compassion is now chastising me publicly for interfering with her peace of mind – and I react instinctively with pain instead of compassion. My exploration of what lies between my current state of being and the state of pure love just went much deeper.

From my interactions and conversations with numerous others here at the nunnery, I know one of the things that

114

exists between some people's state of being and the state of pure love is a lack of ability or willingness to compassionately understand the motives or pain or divinity of others. I do not lack this ability or willingness; I usually have it in spades. But what I realize through this impromptu lesson with Chatterbox is that in times of unexpected confrontation or conflict, I cannot yet react *instinctively* with compassion because I snag first on my own shame-triggered pain. Without anything prompting the sources of my reactionary pain to surface while I am in retreat I cannot see or sense or try to resolve deeply embedded emotional obstacles no matter how long I explore pure love in isolation.

I recall once hearing someone say, "Life is not a race. It's a demolition derby." This is surely applicable to the spiritual journey, because I run into a lot of old junk on this path. And I must, for these things are both the obstructions and the steppingstones on the way to seeing the fullness of truth of who I am. But the way to demolish these pieces of old junk is not to literally bash the hell of them through aggression, negativity or defensiveness. Nor does it work to just keep going around them pretending I do not see them. Instead I must be willing to dig deep and transmute their energy from pain to love.

I have been told many times that I must have a lot of courage to go into isolation and focus internally without distraction. It is true, looking at the inner workings of oneself can be a scary prospect. But I realize now that it also takes a lot of courage to acknowledge and try to transmute what the world "out there" reflects or triggers in me. This is perhaps where some of my hardest and most important work is, for habitual thinking related to old pain is extremely hard to recognize and own up to, never mind transmute. But transmute these things I must, for everything I seek to know, do and be depends on it. So I will dig deep and try to welcome chatterboxes of every sort, for as I seek to unfold fully to truth they too will surely help me develop a compassionate understanding of, and unconditional love for, both others and myself.

Chapter 29

I am reviewing a comment from my very first insight in which, during the crucifixion, I (in/as Jesus) had said, "This was to have been the point of reconciliation." I am reviewing this now after being swept up in the arms of Jesus, then into his body, then integrated into the higher Christ consciousness. I am part of a massive collective consciousness spanning all dimensions. I/We take up much of the cosmos and the sky and are descending slowly over and into Earth.

As I look out over parts of Earth, I speak as Jesus within this consciousness and say in reference to the time of "my" death, "We could have ended things then...the peace and goodness of the earth could have been... but Man made a choice..."

I talk at length now about Man choosing himself over God. "This battle, Man's battle, has always been about Man's will over God's gifts," I say. "None of what we see in this world that is apart from peace ever had to be. Ever. As long as we continue to choose Man's will over God's gifts, it will always feel bad."

I shape two O's in the air by touching my thumbs to my curled fingers on each hand. As I bring my hands together to form one large O I say, "Visually, the point of reconciliation was supposed to have gone like this, where we are separate and then come together as one."

I pull my hands apart and form the two O's again. I

hesitate, then push them together solidly and say, "But what happened was we came together and went like this," then bounce the circles off and away from each other.

I raise the circle of my left hand. "This is Mankind," I say firmly. Then I raise the circle of my right hand. "And this is love and peace and joy and wisdom and caring and kindness."

*"There are pieces that can overlap, but the overwhelming majority exists here," I continue, raising the Mankind circle again. "This is a very hard **conflict**-ridden world."*

I raise the right-hand circle once more. "And this is where we need to be."

I wait for a moment, then add, "In this human existence I have been living in the overlapping portion in the middle of the two O's, and now, I need to be in God's O; I am to reach in and pull people through from Man's O to God's O. That is what I'm supposed to do."

Later I speak about the life of the Jesus that most people think they know. I say, "My existence…was not complicated. But I was not able to reveal that uncomplicatedness in the way that it needed to be revealed so that people could understand it. So people set me apart rather than made me a part of. And I meant to be a part of."

I recall now at the crucifixion seeing the thread of sorrow in the hearts of everyone that continued through to the hearts of everyone today – the sorrow of separation from

God. I say, "The reason [for the continuation of sorrow] is because I, Christ, wasn't in their hearts. I wasn't a part of them to be able to continue. People see me as this distinct separation, and I'm not. Or I wasn't supposed to be."

I speak now about "my" return, which is at hand, and say that this time it will be different. "This time I am not a prophet. I'm... bigger. 'Presence' isn't quite right... bigger. People didn't tell the true story [about my life]. Nobody here has that true story. So in that regard it's not the Second Coming... it's the Coming."

Chapter 30

Many times I have said goodbye to my father as he lay with white sheets pulled up to his chest and medicine trailing through plastic tubes into his weary, scarred body. I have held his needle-pocked hands, kissed the sweat-filled creases of his forehead, and whispered words I hoped would comfort him. And yet he never let go – not yet, not yet, he still had more to speak or do or wish. For twenty years now he could only speak or do or wish feebly, but still, that was enough.

AIDS. Cancer. Congested heart. Blackened lungs. Failing kidneys. Not yet, not yet, not yet.

I cannot be with him to say one more goodbye in person, I am too far away. But I will bow my head and say farewell with a lengthy prayer of thanks in which I recall all the love he gave me and all the moments he made me feel special and smart and beautiful. And in that same prayer I will see for him deep peace and comfort and joy...

News of someone's death, even if it is expected, can suddenly illuminate that person's life in a way it has never before been seen. With the passing of my father today, I realize now this is the illumination of absence.

Chapter 31

Today I have been contemplating what it means to be the light of God. I question whether this has ever been an actual light visible on Earth or if it is simply a radiant goodness that can be sensed through expressions and gestures.

I am warm in my bed and about to fall asleep at the end of this long day when before me comes the answer to my question. In front of my closed eyes comes two "screens" side by side. On one screen is "being God's light" from the experience of my mind. On the other screen is "being God's light" from the experience of my heart.

On the mind screen the scene is drab and extremely elementary. It is like a strange artificial re-creation of a masterpiece depicting everyday life, with simple scenery and stick figure people moving about in predictable, mechanical motion. It is empty of reality, but it is as though the mind is trying earnestly to reproduce its own concept of reality.

Next to this, on the heart screen there is ethereal wonder. Colors are otherworldly and vibrant, with a vibrating clear luminescence simultaneously bathing every single aspect of the scene. Motions of both people and nature are fluid and somehow melodic. Feelings are felt like a breeze and drenched in compassion and understanding. All things in the scene are varying forms of vibration. In fact, the entire scene itself is vibrating, as though the finest movements of the space in which everything exists are visibly alive. In this scene I can see precisely how everything is intertwined. Everything affects everything, and in every impact there are magnificent vibrations of love.

As I watch these two side by side screens, I can see that the heart knows that to be God's light is to let go of all conceptual constraints and BE the full energy, or vibration, of who I Am. And that energy/vibration is all forms of light itself. I can also see that my mind cannot understand what that means – because the very function of my mind is to try to understand, and therefore it can never actually BE or re-produce what it is trying to understand. The mind therefore only – and always –produces a false reality. To be God's light, then, is to BE only – and always – of the heart.

Chapter 32

It is an inviting, inspiring spring day and I must get out of my head and into the beauty.

Under a crisp blue sky I skip ten minutes up the footpath to my favorite tree in the rice fields. I tune to Portuguese fado on my iPod, turn to face the sun, close my eyes and begin to dance. I sway and move my arms and hips in rhythm with the music, then turn to smile at the snowy Himalayas and sway some more with my arms outstretched. Appreciation of this moment is flowing inside me like a rushing river.

When I turn back around to face the sun again, still swaying with my arms outstretched, I open my eyes and see an elderly Indian woman in flowing orange and red colors walking up the footpath. She is smiling and holding her hands together at her forehead in traditional "bless you" greeting. I smile and wave, return the gesture of blessing and continue to dance.

When the woman gets near enough, I meet her on the footpath and hold up one of my iPod ear buds, inviting her to hear what I am dancing to. She nods, leans in close to my head and puts the ear bud in her ear. She looks me square in the eye, smiles even bigger, and starts swaying.

We giggle and sway together for a bit, then she abruptly takes the ear bud out and motions me back to the tree. I smile and bid her goodbye, then head back to the tree dancing with every step. When I get to the tree I turn and see the woman is right behind me. She waves at me to continue dancing then sits down on a large rock and puts the bag she is carrying on her lap. While I dance she reaches into the bag and takes out a bundle of yarn and two long blue needles, tilts her face up toward the warm sun and begins to knit.

Chapter 33

I am in McLeod-ganj visiting His Holiness the Dalai Lama's main temple for the fourth or fifth time. I came here just to walk, pray, contemplate, feel the energy and enjoy the dramatic mountain views.

The first time I saw the interior of His Holiness's temple I was surprised at how small it is. The two main halls are each, I am guessing, only about 50 feet by 150 feet. In the first hall the walls are hand-painted in traditional thangka style using elegant fine lines and handcrafted colors to depict deities and scenes from Buddhist history. Bejeweled Buddha statues are enclosed in glass cases with offerings of money and food placed all around.

In the second, less ornate hall, there are wood-paneled walls and colorful Tibetan tapestries surrounding a modest raised platform upon which His Holiness the Dalai Lama sits to give his teachings.

There are also several large golden statues of revered Buddhist teachers in the second hall. The largest of these is a statue of a young Shakyamuni Buddha, the man said to have attained enlightenment under the pipal tree and who went on to share teachings that would eventually become known as Buddhist dharma. The statue is placed prominently above and behind His Holiness's teaching platform so it looks directly out onto the hall. Having seen hundreds of Buddha statues of all shapes and sizes in my time here in India, and truthfully not being very moved by them, I do not pay close attention to the details of this

Buddha statue today.   Besides, I have already seen it several times before.

I have been standing to the right of this statue for about ten minutes taking in the beauty of the room and thinking about how much peace has been fostered by the intention here. As I make to leave the hall I turn back and look up at the face of the Buddha statue one last time... and suddenly know the young man this person was before he was known as Buddha. Right in the core of my being I feel his spirit and intentions fully alive as though they are my own. I do not just know what he represents, I know <u>him</u>. And I know he is filled with <u>profound</u> kindness and compassion for all beings. I stand staring at the statue for another minute or so, fully absorbed in the eternal energy of young Buddha.

By nightfall I am fatigued from the events of the day. It is always tiring to go up the mountain to the crowded, cold, messy little town of McLeod-ganj, and today's unexpected event drained a lot more of my energy after I spent several hours amped up with elation.

Before going to sleep I decide to spend a little time relaxing with friends online. We are roaring with laughter over the fact that Buddhist nuns' heads are shaped like the letter O. We are making up silly "nun scenes" playing off the letter O, for example: O- O- O- O- is a group of nuns holding their plates in a lunch line; iO is Apple's Buddhist work group; 8 is a former nun, now a model. I am so tired everything is hysterically funny, and I cannot remember the last time I laughed this hard.

128

Finally I am ready for sleep, so I shut my computer down and curl up under the covers layered in my long underwear, two sets of pajamas, socks and a hat. As soon as I close my eyes in this wonderfully open, grateful and joyful state, quick as a blink ALL the lessons of my visions and insights for all these years suddenly come together. Finally, on a cold night in the rice fields of India as I lay smiling and shivering in my little twin bed, I get IT.

And by IT, I mean the meaning of life.

By IT I mean I understand what Jesus and Buddha knew and how their teachings fit together to give the full picture of how we got here, what we are doing here, where we are going, and how to get there.

I now know what I am doing here in India. I know what I am doing here in this world. And I know what I am supposed to do with all I understand.

I just have no idea how to do it or how to put it into words.

Chapter 34

For the last three days I have awakened from a deep sleep at 4:44 AM. The first morning, after having zero inspiration to write for three weeks, I woke up with a powerful urge to write about what I know of the meaning of life. This morning I woke up with a powerful urge to have a *beautiful* day.

So I thought it would be nice to start my beautiful day off with a one-hour walk at sunrise. As I am weaving my way through the terraced fields that surround the nunnery, two large snowy white birds fly slowly and very low right in front of me – literally within a few feet. The body of the birds is instantly familiar but I cannot register what kind of birds they are because I have never seen pure white like that except on a swan or an egret. Shortly it dawns on me the birds were ravens. Two. White. Ravens.

Minutes later I turn onto the dirt path leading to the village and come upon a haphazard stream of toddling Tibetan kids sleepily walking to "daycare school" about a mile from the community center where they live. As I pass two little girls holding hands and shuffling along with their heads down, I look back and see the smallest girl, who is at most three years old, raise her head. I smile over my shoulder and move my fingers up and down in a wave behind my back to say hi. But I have forgotten that this gesture means "come here" to them instead of "hello." As my mistake is dawning on me, the tiny girl is quickening her step and reaching up to take hold of my hand. So I slow my pace wayyy down and walk two sleepy little girls to school.

My walk back then takes me past the home of the nunnery's cleaning lady, Anu. Anu's young daughter, Shabu, suffered severe burns in an electrical fire two months ago and for three weeks I spent countless hours in intensive care and the rural health clinic helping Anu maneuver the maze of medical, financial and logistical complications she faced trying to save Shabu's foot and leg.

The last time I saw Shabu, which was nearly a month ago because of my retreat schedule, she was still going the clinic three days a week for skin treatment and physical therapy, but she was stable – she could move her toes and put part of her heel down at an angle to awkwardly limp short distances. Today as I round the corner of her house, Shabu sees me from the porch where she stands in her bare feet, sweeping. She instantly beams a huge smile and says, "Mary didi!" (Aunt Mary). Then she walks toward me with a gorgeously even stride to give me a warm, teary hug.

No matter what happens from now until bedtime, this is a *beautiful* day.

132

Chapter 35

For my birthday my friend and fellow nunnery resident, Mudita, has for weeks been excited about the prospect of taking me to what is supposed to be a particularly beautiful area of the Himalayas a couple of hours north of the nunnery. It is very secluded and known to have a few cabins and caves where people sometimes go for remote spiritual retreats. The location is accessible only by a long hike from a dirt road.

It is around midnight the night before our outing and I am just drifting off to sleep when a vision comes into my mind's eye. I see Mudita and I hiking on the way to the cabins. We are walking down a bank toward a bridge that spans a small stream when five young Indian men come out from beneath the bridge and run up the bank to viciously attack us.

This fearful vision comes as a surprise to me since most mornings Mudita and I hike in the mountains for several hours, and have even sat in meditation in remote areas, and we have never once had any fear of being attacked. I can feel that in no uncertain terms my vision is a premonition: we are not to go on this hike.

I know Mudita will be asleep so I send her a text message telling her I do not think we should go on the trip as planned and I will explain in the morning. Minutes later Mudita knocks on my door. "I just had a nightmare, Mary, and it was bad," she says, visibly shaken. "We were attacked in the mountains by a group of men while we were hiking tomorrow. I don't think we should go."

She has no idea about my vision. I say, "Oh my God, I just had a vision of the same thing!"

She goes on, anxiously: "Oh God! In my dream we were by a stream and five village-looking guys came up the bank and attacked us. It was so real, Mary! We can't go!"

We compare notes on the guys, the stream, the bridge, the attack... all the same.

Needless to say, we do not go. Instead she takes me to an abandoned fort that is now a national park about two hours the opposite direction from our original destination.

In the evening when we return from the fort, on her way to her room Mudita runs into Sangmo, the founder and abbess of Thosamling. Sangmo mistakenly thinks our outing to the cabins was planned for tomorrow. She stops Mudita and says, "I've been looking for you. I have a bad feeling about your trip. I don't think you should go."

Chapter 36

I have been battling a lonely state of mind for a while now. I have tried repeatedly and cannot seem to put my wordless knowledge into words. And yet I must, otherwise I will surely smother to death under this heavy weight of vast wordlessness. I look around at the pretty surroundings and try to feel better, but it is no use.

The nunnery put up new Tibetan prayer flags. They are pretty. And I am still lonely.

The mustard plants are blooming in the fields. They are pretty. And I am still lonely.

I look out at this monastery from my window. It is pretty. And I am still lonely.

Today in this monastery I have an appointment I am very much looking forward to with a highly revered eighty-five-year-old teacher known widely in Tibet and India for his oracle abilities. He is the former secretary of the Department of Religious Affairs for the Tibeten Government-in-Exile and was one of the Dalai Lama's primary teachers for more than thirty years. It is clear from his kind eyes and patient speech that he is still comfortable and content sharing his wisdom.

In a long stately room filled with Buddha status and richly brocade Tibetan tapestries, I sit on a thick blue carpet in front of His Holiness Garje Khamtrul Rinpoche for one and a quarter hours discussing, through a translator, the nature of my insights and abilities. Abbess Sangmo-la sits silently beside me for support. It is she who worked for five weeks to arrange this meeting on my behalf.

I want two things from this meeting: assistance with my meditation techniques and, most importantly, permission to work with the Rinpoche so he can help me process what I know and begin to shape it into words. Sangmo is certain he is the best man to help me.

We begin with a lengthy discussion about the nature of my visions and insights. The Rinpoche wants to know about the general theme of the visions and if I am looking at or absorbed in what I see. Are the senses engaged? Is there time? Can I go to other realms on command? I answer his questions as best I can and make sure he understands that things also come to me not only in visions but in sudden insights of clear "knowing." He listens and nods patiently.

I finally show the translator a crude drawing and explain that this is what I know of the entire continuum of life/existence. I point to a small dot on the left side of the page and say, "Please tell him this is me at the very first moment I was aware of consciousness."

The translator says, very matter of factly, "You mean in this lifetime."

138

"No. I mean ever. I know the first moment I had consciousness." As I explain the rest of the drawing I add, "And this is the evolution of my *being* from that point."

The Rinpoche takes off the glasses he is wearing and puts on a pair of reading glasses to study the drawing carefully. He asks several questions to clarify his understanding and nods pensively with each answer I give. Finally, he takes off his reading glasses and slowly puts back on his other pair. He looks at me solemnly, pauses to gather his words thoughtfully, and then says, "What you know is what we call the primordial ground. It is the origin of life before beginning; it is before 'arising'; it is before concept... and as such it is beyond words. It is the realm beyond words. Whatever words I have to tell you, you already know. You already know more than I can teach, and I can be of no use to you."

Whoa. I cannot even take in the scope of what he is saying, it feels so unreal. Instead I focus on the "I can be of no use to you." I quickly explain that I have been shown many times that my "work" is specifically to shape my knowledge into words in order to help end suffering for all beings, so surely there must be a way. He offers a few kind words of advice on *what* to share with others: "People cannot always hear, and not everyone can hear the same thing. See what they are ready to hear and share that much." Then he surprises me by adding, "But we must also accept that we may not be able to help many others. Greater people than the four of us in the room have not been able to heal this world's suffering. Buddha could not pull us out. Jesus could not pull us out. So we should help who we can, directly or indirectly, and accept that may be all we can do in this lifetime."

I have a million things I want to say, but the only words that come to my lips are, "It has been a blessing to have this time with you. Thank you so much for seeing me." But then I remember he has not answered my request for help with my meditations. I say, "Oh, but can you advise me on my meditation technique so I can at least seek more guidance that way?

He shakes his head. "No. Truth comes to you already in its own way. That is how is has to be."

Sangmo-la and I walk back to the nunnery in silence. We go into the dining hall to put on hot water for tea and while the water is heating we both stand with our backs against the counter and our arms crossed, staring at the floor while we wordlessly process the outcome of the meeting. Finally I say, "You know, I don't really drink the stuff much, but a shot of whiskey sounds really good right now." She looks at me out of the corner of her eye and says, "There's a bottle in the office. I would understand." (She says a resident left it as a prayer offering, of all things.)

So once again I sit alone now on my little twin bed with a head full of knowledge I do not know how to convey and a heart full of passionate desire to convey it. I am caught in the paradox of having knowledge without words and a life purpose of using words to share my knowledge.

Sangmo-la is very willing to help me but like me has no idea what that help needs to be. So for now the only resource I have for help is my mind and that wordless truth that is trying hard to make its way out into the world through me. I have to trust it will happen eventually, and when it does I feel it only appropriate to plan on toasting that big ol' truth with a big ol' shot of contraband whiskey.

.

Chapter 37

I am trying to understand the relationship between thought and form. How was I able to begin my evolution with just a thought? What is the nature of a single "particle" of thought?

I ask these questions generally to the universe as I am sitting on my bed looking out the window. I have been thinking about this subject all afternoon and now I grow deeply tired and feel the need for a nap. Almost as soon as I lay back on my pillow a gorgeous symmetrical pattern of rotating atom-like energies comes before me.

The energies are bright like aluminum lit in sunlight and mirror-like reflective. As I watch these energies move together in various patterns, one "atom" moves forward so I can see it in exquisite detail. The center looks like a ring of flower petals rotating counter-clockwise. Surrounding these petals are several circular rows of identical square plates, the edge of each slightly propped up on the other. The rows of plates are all rotating clockwise. The last plate on the outer edge is an image of me, happily smiling and waving.

I understand as I look at this design that I create my perception of physical form through the reflective interaction of the inner petals and outer plates. Energy from the center (the thought) reflects onto the energies rotating around it (mirrors) and then bit-by-bit builds hologram-like reflections back and forth, back and forth...until the reflection finally transmutes my thoughts into perceptions in physical form.

144

As I consider this image my understanding expands enormously. I can now see how mankind has built the world we live in throughout evolution. We have expanded our reflective energies with every new experience: we think, create, learn and expand, think, create, learn and expand. Along the way we develop numerous senses and modes of intellect to help us perceive more and learn more, and in doing so we create a perception of time and space.

We begin to intellectualize more and more as we discern "this" from "that" and "I" from "other," and as we do so we begin interpreting our existence in terms of contrast and concepts. (If we are red and our whole environment is red, we can only experience red when we encounter the contrast of, say, yellow.) Our big leap comes when contrast leads to the concept of conflict. We had begun this evolutionary journey with the concept of "this is good/me, that is different than good/me" and now change to the concept of "this is good/me, that is <u>bad</u>." And we experience this bad as threatening, which leads to the experience of fear. And it is fear that inherently creates a false belief that there is existence other than Love. Today we know this false existence of separation from Love as Ego. Ego is entirely fear-based and fear-fed.

Our original intention was to experience our BEing of goodness by understanding what it is to BE with that which feels like our own goodness and what it is to BE with that which feels different from our own goodness – which is BEing through contrast. This kind of BEing through experience was rooted in good, innocent and eager intentions. But as I watch us evolve to experience judgment with that contrast, I see us make a critical turn away from remembering our Divine nature as joyful BEings. Our thoughts begin to focus on our BEing in the conflict of good-versus-bad instead of focusing on the joyful experience of contrast. And since our thoughts create the energy that creates our world, good-versus-bad become the foundation of the world we live in today.

Chapter 38

I wake up to a vision of Gandhi, Mother Teresa, Buddha and Jesus all walking past me one by one in a straight line. As each one passes in front of me they say, "We only did what we *knew.*"

So over coffee and oatmeal, I think about what it is exactly that I *know* – not in my mind but in my heart, in the depths of my soul.

I know that in the beginning there was the expansive darkness of God, which is all and only Love. In this exquisite Love cosmos, which is the endless pure potential of everything, Love united with a massive field of latent energy. When this happened the latent energy became "charged" with Love, and conscious life began. All life then became possible through energy, and every kind of energy became possible. All life *exists* through Love-engorged energy.

I know this. But what do I do with this knowledge?

I know that in the Love energy cosmos, which is accessible only within us, there is the fundamental Law of Equality governing unconditional love. *Everything has potential, all potential is possible, and every potential and possibility is equal.* Suffering arises from any manner of inequality, for judgment of any kind is out of alignment with that which governs unconditional Love.

I know this. But what do I do with this knowledge?

I know that I, like every form of life, am a complex compilation of, or unique frequency of, vibrations of Love energy with a fundamental desire to *become through experience* the fullness of who I really am – which is Love.

I know this. But what do I do with this knowledge?

I know that the fundamental feeling at the core of Love is Joy. The fundamental joyful experience of BEing Love is the experience of Goodness – or *Godness*. I know that at the very core of our BEing *every human being knows we are all God's/Love's goodness* but we have long forgotten this truth. I also know that to progress evermore toward BEing the full potential of our true goodness – our Godness – is our purpose in life.

I know this. But what do I do with this knowledge?

I know the first thought I ever had in the history of my existence was: *I am goodness and want to BE all that I Am!* And I know this thought propelled me with great force into my evolution of BEing. I *felt* my thought as the energy propelling me. I also know that my thinking mind creates a perception of reality that is not, in fact, actual reality. The world I see all around simply *reflects my thought-driven perception* of physical form-based reality. The entire "normal" existence in which I live is the interplay of energies working together to reflect back every thought, including sub-conscious and unconscious thoughts as well as the collective thoughts of the masses, since we are simultaneously One and All.

I know this. But what do I do with this knowledge?

148

I know that I experience Christ as the consciousness of purely compassionate Love-centered intention. The energy of the Christ consciousness includes an unfathomable number of beings, including Jesus, Buddha and myself, and we all hold unique but interwoven roles within the collective. I experience Jesus as the primary force of Christ/Christ consciousness, and Buddha as both an integral part and a broader expansion of same. I also know that Buddha and Jesus share the exact same compassionate intentions to free all beings from suffering and both are in agreement that freedom from suffering comes from clearing the mind, purifying the heart and understanding Divine wisdom. I share their intentions and understandings, but much of the written teachings and practices of Buddhism and Christianity do not resonate with me. So what do I do with my knowledge of Buddha and Jesus?

Every day the question of what to do with this knowledge, what to do with this knowledge, what to do with this knowledge trails behind me wherever I go. Even today, as Gandhi, Mother Theresa, Buddha and Jesus pass by reminding me to look at what I know, I think: Okay, I know these things...but so what? What. Do. I. Do. With. This. Knowledge?

Chapter 39

I am standing on a road made entirely of pure truth. I stand upon this road as a body of light made of the same pure truth. All the people of the world are behind me and I am about to lead them down this road.

In my physical body I feel pressure from a bolus of energy stuck in my chest. I focus on the area just below the block and imagine forcing the obstruction to move or dissolve. While doing this I become so nauseated I have to fetch a bowl and paper towel in case I throw up. I try now to be still and just let the energy do what it will. Shortly I feel movement in my chest and with astonishing clarity I become both the image and the wisdom of the image of the road of pure truth, my own light of pure truth and the world behind me that I am about to lead onto this road.

I Am the Way, the Truth, and the <u>Light</u>.

Chapter 40

Today I am feeling hopeful. I have been reading about a fascinating young artist, and as I read I feel many levels of insight kicking in at once to show how the world is changing. This is a new kind of knowing for me; it is not a vision or a specific-subject insight as much as a vast and acute understanding of current global conditions.

This understanding begins first with the vital importance of the connection between mind and physical body. Throughout history there have been thousands of documented accounts of people encountering Divine realms during surgery, meditation, illness, accident, etc. and all these stories share one key fact: the physical bodies remained right here on Earth. Through the physical vessel we are all an integral part of the Divine realms *all the time, right where we are*, but our fear-trained minds are conditioned not to perceive it. However, I know a powerful change in this conditioning is very much at hand.

The extraordinary young artist I have been reading about is Akiane Kramarik. Akiane says that at the age of four she began being inspired by God to write poetry and paint. At the age of eight she painted one of two "Jesus" works, including this one entitled *Prince of Peace*.

Akiane paints primarily from inspiration in her visions, dreams and conversations with God. At the age of sixteen, she painted a work called *Tomorrow*, and for me this perfectly portrays the exhilarating state into which we are heading.

I recognize in this painting an awakening of the physical form to the presence of much higher energy vibrations I myself have stood in and watched as my entire surroundings transformed from trees and rocks and air to a spectacular all-encompassing vibrations of joy that were very much alive.

I know all life on Earth to be in this field of joyful vibration at all times – indeed we are all part of it – and yet most of us usually cannot sense it. We cannot sense this joyful vibration because we live in the world we built on thoughts of conflict, which is a very different kind of energy vibration. It is like we are tuned into an AM radio signal of good-versus-bad when Divine joy is a completely different FM signal of All Is Love.

For thousands of years humans have been indoctrinating each other over and over again with the notion that conflict is a necessary and integral part of life, and most effectively using God as proof of its value. When in fact, it is not necessary at all. We have just *been thinking* it is. The more we have thought in terms of conflict, the more we have built a world out of it. And the more we have built a world out of thoughts of conflict, the further away from our natural state of absolute love and peace we have grown – it does not matter whether we look at it from a global, religious, cultural, monetary, community, individual or any other basis.

The list of pervasive conflicts that hold us in steady dissonance with the joy of the Divine realms is long, starting with the inability to forgive, greed, aggression, judgment, and cultural/political/religious efforts to mold individuals and societies into that which is against our true nature. The bottom line is that we live in a world ruled by the *thought* of conflict, and that keeps us from the reality that is ruled by the truth of Love.

But today I can see that the eons of time we have spent thinking in terms of conflict have also allowed us the time to finally begin remembering our way back to our joyful intentions. I know without question I am here in this human form writing these words now because I remember. And I am realizing that I am not alone.

I look at the entire planet today and see more people slowly waking up, turning to peaceful options and getting closer to remembering. I see more individuals thinking about what feels spiritually right *to them* and finding the will to go in that direction. I see prejudices tilting toward equality in small and enormously significant ways. I see courageous youth rising up not from a desire for power but from a desire for equality. I see media teaching people over and over and over again how bad the barrage of conflict feels, and I see we are slowly, slowly learning that lesson. I see an entire globe filling up with young, confident, hopeful energy that says *of course* conflict is not helpful, and they are talking about it with each other on social networks in every corner of the globe.

And I see young Akiane Kramarik painting *Tomorrow* because she too knows our time of remembering is at hand.

More and more, I can see we are *thinking* differently as a world. We are thinking more lovingly, more peacefully, more inclusively, more joyfully despite being shouted at incessantly by the media and religious and political leaders telling us the world is going to hell in a hand basket and it is all a sure sign of Armageddon.

Today I know change *is* coming and it is not the conflict-centered, fear-driven story of Armageddon. It is love like we have never dared to imagine. I see this love with absolute certainty: it *is* coming. In fact, it is *arriving* more and more every day. It is arriving in me and in Akiane and in people everywhere. And on some level we all want to wake up and welcome it.

Chapter 41

I am in a strange place between a dream and a vision. I am not asleep but I am also not awake.

I approach a large cement circle with a fire pit in the center where a large gold-white fire is burning. In the upper left corner from where I sit a golden bridge appears and Buddha walks across and sits down on a bench in front of the fire. Another bridge forms in the upper right corner and Jesus walks across and sits down. Shortly many bridges form and others gather round, though they are quite faint and I cannot make them out clearly.

Shortly a strong elderly Native American chief approaches from the other side of Jesus, bends over and knocks his tomahawk onto the cement several times until it breaks. This is to signify peace, ridding the present moment of any past reputations. The chief then turns and walks away.

Next comes Pope Francis, looking old and rather haggard from carrying a load too heavy to bear. He takes out his Bible and knocks it repeatedly against the cement until the upper half of the book breaks off. He keeps hold of the remaining bottom half, though still not happy with it, and walks away.

Next comes a very elderly man dressed all in white. He is being helped to the circle by two winged angels, also in white. I understand this is Father Time. When he approaches the circle he takes off his glasses, puts them on the cement by the fire, and steps on them, smashing them to little pieces. He no longer needs to see time. He then walks all the way around the circle, still aided by the angels but much sturdier, and then walks away.

Buddha and Jesus are still gathered here, as am I. We all come to the edge of the circle, bend down and silently pray. Shortly Buddha stands up and takes off his khata (ceremonial scarf) and drops it in the same place where the others have broken their items. He is ridding himself of ritual, which serves no purpose now.

Jesus then takes off his sandals and places them with Buddha's khata. He does this to indicate that we no longer need to walk this long road. We are ready to fly.

Chapter 42

Back when I first arrived in India, His Holiness the 17th Karmapa had wisely instructed me to "slowly, slowly" take the time to learn who I am. The most important thing I have learned thus far in this journey is what it means to be The Message of Christ. Not the messenger, *The Message*. I understand now, in the deepest reaches of my soul, my role here on Earth is not to tell of the resurrection of Christ. My role is to *embody* it. I am a light of and for the return of the Christ consciousness, both announcing its arrival and illuminating its way.

But if embodying the words of Christ were easy I would be a blinding beacon of light already. I must confess that as I have tried to figure out how to do what is asked of me I have learned a valuable lesson about the meaning of: *"This battle, Man's battle, has always been about Man's will over God's gifts."*

I left India during monsoon season in summer 2012. I intended to be in the U.S. for three months to visit friends and family and to officiate a wedding, but that three months turned into a year and a half. In retrospect, as I evaluate what my intentions were with a painful measure of honesty, I realize I had tried to turn my "slowly, slowly" into "quickly, quickly." I did not want to just visit family and friends. I thought I might be ready to incorporate my spiritual work into some semblance of a normal life again. I could call this a mistake, but I think it is more correct to call it a 'tough love' lesson that proved my work is not to be taken lightly.

That trip was ill fated right off the bat. The first night I was back in the States, as I slept in my best friend Reese's guest bedroom, a strong storm raged through the area knocking down trees and power lines. The next morning while on a walk I stepped around a lot of debris and occasionally into, I realized too late, poison ivy. I was wearing sandals and had on my right ankle a brand new delicately designed charm bracelet tattoo that I had gotten as a special treat for myself in Delhi just hours before catching my flight.

The following day telltale signs of poison ivy cropped up on both feet and ankles, and the all too familiar itch of allergic reaction began. That afternoon as I headed to Virginia to visit my ex-girlfriend Mary, my right ankle began to swell. The next day the poison ivy spots on my left foot and ankle were normal but the ones on my right had begun to redden around the edges. Within twenty-four hours my right calf turned red and I began having trouble walking, so I went to the doctor. It turns out that poison ivy oil mixed with fresh tattoo ink is a dangerous combination and I was fast developing a serious staph infection.

The first round of medications did not work. The next day my leg from the knee down was swollen and I could not touch my toe to the ground without pain. The infection spread rapidly; my muscles grew stiff and the poison ivy spots turned into angry white pustules bordered in deep red. I returned to see the doctor again.

The second round of medications did not work. The pain deepened into my muscles and bones all the way up to my

162

rear end. I could not put my foot down flat and any standing pressure was extremely painful. More than fifty pustules encircled my lower leg and were climbing up my calf.

I saw the doctor again for the third time in four days. This time he said "If you don't see any results from these meds in the next twenty-four hours we're going to have to get you on IV antibiotics ASAP."

By the following morning I could tell the infection had at least not gotten worse; the meds appear to be working. Over the next few days the pain gradually subsided everywhere but my lower calf and foot. I still could not easily walk and the pustules were hideous, but there was definite improvement. I spent another seven days much as I had the previous four, sitting with my leg elevated on a pillow.

Although the unexpected infection was unsightly and inconvenient, I was happy that at least my stationary convalescence allowed me time to work on a talk I was going to give alongside my friend and former therapist Margery a few days after I headed back to DC to visit more friends. Margery and I had started planning this talk before I left India, thinking it would be good to share my story and the story of our work together in hopes of inspiring or helping other therapists and patients. Margery had titled the talk: *From Spiritual Emergency to Spiritual Emergence: Conversation With an Unwitting Mystic.* In preparation for the event she had sent out the following notice:

Dear Friends and Colleagues,

Through the art, science, and poetry of the therapeutic relationship, we are often as transformed by our patients as they are by us. This was and still is certainly the case with my relationship with Mary Reed. Mary has given me permission to speak of our therapy, which was less like therapy and more like mid-wifery to the birth of a powerful new Being, whose life force and direction took us both by surprise.

Last year, Mary came to me in a state of emotional crisis. She was several weeks past a serious suicide attempt. Thank goodness, she was not successful. I will not go into the details of that part of our journey together, and will leave that part of the story up to her.

I will let you know that, in the course of our work together, she received a surprise invitation to go to India and study with the Dalai Lama. She accepted the invitation, got rid of everything that defined her life in the United States, and began her spiritual studies in India. We continued to stay in touch through her brilliantly written Blog. It was her goal to integrate the various mystical visions that had taken hold of her and had originally been so compelling, so frightening and so confusing. Now, she has recently returned to the United States and wants to share with others what she has learned about the nature of Consciousness and how she has integrated those mystical understandings about our Ultimate Purpose. Mary is gifted in her ability to speak in straightforward and humorous language about "The Way We Are."

I am very grateful to have been part of her spiritual journey and would like to offer this special invitation to hear her speak.

164

Registration filled up quickly; the event would be standing room only at a lovely waterside community center in Annapolis, Maryland.

The night before the talk I was again staying at Reese's house and had an odd all-over headache I could not seem to shake. It felt like pressure radiating from the inside center of my head outward in all directions. I slept poorly and woke up in the morning feeling much worse. I could not stand upright without feeling like I was going to pass out. I tried everything I could think of to shake it off – tea, meditation, Tylenol, sinus tablet, and nothing worked. I spent the day in bed trying with every ounce of strength I had to will the pain away.

I was supposed to leave at 6:00 PM for the talk. At 5:00 PM Reese came home from work to find me lying in the bed, flushed and sweaty. I told her my whole head felt like it was trying to burst. She took my temperature: 103. "Honey, I have to take you to the hospital," she said.

While Reese was helping me get ready I called Margery to let her know I would not be able to make it to the talk. I wanted to cry while talking to her but I did not have the strength. I just said, "I am so, so sorry."

In the emergency room a nurse took me back for examination in a triage room within minutes. Everything was too bright and the lights swirled in my line of sight as the nurse helped me into a large blue recliner. My head hurt worse than I thought was even possible. An older Middle Eastern-looking man with a dark moustache and receding hairline was the first doctor to examine me. "Have you had fever or headache before today?" he asked as he looked in my eyes with a pin light.

"The headache started last night and the fever came earlier today," I replied. "But I did have a bad staph infection in my leg recently and just finished my meds for that a couple of days ago."

He listened to my heart and lungs, then put on a pair of gloves and examined the pustules still prevalent around my leg, bending my foot and knee in the process to check for stiffness. While he was looking my leg over he said, "I understand you live in India? Did you have any health trouble over there? How long have you been back in the states?"

"I've been back almost three weeks," I said in a weak whisper. "I was in great health over there, then got the staph infection right after I arrived in the states because I got poison ivy on my new tattoo." The doctor nodded with sincere concern, putting pieces together one by one in his head. He ordered several lab tests and said he would see me again shortly.

After the first tubes of blood were drawn I could no longer sit up. A nurse transferred me via wheelchair to a bed in the emergency care area. For the next six hours one doctor after another came to examine me and ask questions. I repeated over and over that I had had a recent staph infection and that I had been in India for nine months and had no unusual health problems while there. I told them about the prescription drug overdose the previous year during my suicide attempt and about some of the health complications in my history. "No, I do not take illegal drugs," I told them. "No, I am not on any prescription drugs at this time. No, to my knowledge I have not been bitten by anything. No, I was not in a malaria-prone region of India."

They gave me aspirin, then something stronger, then eventually morphine trying to ease the pain; nothing worked. The fever, too, persisted. They ran more blood tests and transferred me back and forth from room to room, bed to gurney, gurney to machine, gurney to bed as they performed scans and x-rays and eventually a spinal tap. Every move felt like it was going to crack my skull open. Every test revealed nothing as to the source of the problem.

They admitted me to the sixth floor for further evaluation. The intense pain, fever, questions and tests continued for days. They ruled out Yellow Fever, Dengue Fever, malaria, viral meningitis, bacterial meningitis, systemic staph, tumors and myriad other possibilities. No one had any idea what was going on and neither did I.

Reese, Mary and my friend Nan all took turns visiting me but I was so doped up and so tired from lack of sleep due to pain that I did not retain much memory of what we spoke about or how long they were with me. I did, however, stay alert enough one evening to know that Mary was bathing me with a cold washcloth. I cried both from the relief of coolness against my skin and the comfort of nurturing tenderness with which it was applied.

One evening – or morning? – I looked to my left and saw Margery at my bedside sitting in a chair. I did not retain what she said about how she found me but I recalled her saying with such sweet kindness, "We had to cancel the event, but the staff of the center did a prayer circle for you. Everyone is sending you love and lots of healing energy." This, too, made me cry.

While I was aware during that time that I was very ill, I was also aware that I was not going to die. I did not believe I had survived a suicide attempt one year just to die of a brain infection the next. Nor did I believe that God and my whole Divine gang went through all the trouble training me for so long just to say "oh never mind" then. Through the fog of drugs and pain I wondered what the higher purpose in such an unexpected trial could possibly be, but trusted that whatever it was I just needed to tough the moment out. And I was right.

On the fifth day the head pain began to subside and the fever gradually disappeared. That evening my appetite returned and by the next afternoon I was able to stand long enough to shower. By the seventh day I could not tolerate the idea of lying in the bed any longer and requested to leave. The doctors said I was too weak to be released and they still wanted to monitor me and run more tests, but I knew without a doubt my healing was on course. That evening I walked out of the hospital flanked by my rescuers Reese and Nan.

The week I was in the hospital happened to be the exact week I was supposed to visit my family in Texas; I was to catch a flight to Dallas the day after my talk. My sister had taken three days off work and my brother had made plans to take me camping. It would have been the first time I had seen my siblings in nearly two years and the first time we would all be together since our father's passing. But the visit was not to be.

The snowball of trouble continued to expand. The talk I was to give with Margery was a donation-based event and I had hoped to network with the professionals there for other potential speaking or even teaching possibilities that might generate income. Without any source of financial support the pressures began to mount.

Due to my already costly illnesses and slow recovery, flights had to be rerouted which cost money I had not budgeted to spend. A budding friendship-turned-romance was snipped off abruptly and I ended up staying at a hotel for several days because I had nowhere else to go before I was due at the wedding I would officiate. My health (mental and physical) had not quite recovered enough to return to India on the appointed date, so I ended up staying with friends for a few months before landing a seasonal on-site residency job at a spiritual retreat center in New Mexico. There I was immediately caught in the tail end of a fifteen-year escalation of workplace bullying that came to a head in a staff walkout just weeks after I arrived. When I decided to return to India and scrape by on extremely low funds, I found the airline's policies had changed and my return ticket was no longer valid.

During this wildly frustrating period I tried several times to put words to my visions and insights in the form of a book. But every time my efforts were halting and stilted, as though I was trying to choke the words out against their will. Unable to move any spiritual work to the forefront amid this chaos, I found myself once again stuck in an all too familiar place between the crush of failures and financial pressures in the "normal" world and an inability to know what to do with my spiritual knowledge.

This time, however, I knew better than to give in to the confusion and depression. So, just like I did nearly three years prior, I surrendered completely once again. My sister invited me to her house to stay as long as I needed and I accepted gratefully. I stopped trying to make any further plans. I stopped worrying. I stopped trying to control my direction. It was nearing the holiday season and I knew I would get to be with family I had not seen in years, so I stayed focused on how blessed I was with the timing of my current situation and just let everything else go. And every day I prayed, "Dear God, I turn this over to you. You can see once again I have no idea what I am doing. Please show me the way."

While in that place of surrender, one afternoon I recalled the day when I had awakened to the vision of Gandhi, Mother Theresa, Jesus and Buddha all walking past me saying, "We only did what we *knew*." It suddenly occurred to me that I did not have to know what "to do" with what I have been shown – because that is not what I know. *What* I know is *all* I know. That very day I began to write with ease, simply recounting the metaphysical events as they actually happened and foregoing any narrative interpretation or explanation about what they mean. I was certain I was heading in the right direction when a new kind of experience began to happen.

Within just a few hours of working on the new manuscript, a formless, transparent spirit appeared before me. It felt like an adoring grandmother, a wise guardian and an ornery childhood friend all rolled up into one. The spirit cupped my cheeks in its "hands" and said very excitedly, "Yes, yes!" It was powerfully encouraging and upbeat energy, and thrilled me so deeply I had to squinch my face up to absorb all the joy. The spirit appeared in the exact same way again and again, at least thirty times over the next few months, always at a time when I was working on something I felt needed to be handled particularly delicately. It was like a cheerleader keeping me company and a monitor keeping me on track.

As soon as I had an early draft of the manuscript ready I passed it along to my dear friend Barbara, a former Roman Catholic nun and still devoutly active member of the Catholic Church. Over the previous year Barbara had become a spiritual confidante, sharing stories of Christian mystics and explaining to me the many ways she sees that my experiences are supported by history and scripture. She had reviewed some of my previous writing and, like me, was excited to see the changes in my new work.

Barbara wisely reminded me that, just as Margery Silverton and Dr. Bauer had advised me early on, what I needed most was to be in a supportive community where I could focus on my spiritual work in quietude. After lengthy deliberation and research, I decided my best option was to figure out a way to return to India. The moment that decision was firm in my mind, the spirit appeared again, cupping my cheeks and excitedly saying, "Yes, yes!"

It was my devoutly Catholic friend Barbara, along with two other devoutly Catholic friends named Barbara and a few other friends who have followed my journey, who through generosity and love made it possible for me to book my flight back to the Buddhist nunnery. When I finalized the airline reservation and the confirmation popped up on my computer screen, the spirit appeared once again, this time laughing joyfully. It raised its "hands" up, tousled my hair, and playfully kissed the top of my head. Beaming with love, it then said, "See you there!"

Chapter 43

Three nights ago I began including in my pre-sleep prayer something to the effect of, "May I do work in this night that will be of DEEP benefit to myself and the universe in this time." (A slightly different version of my routine nightly prayer.) Each night since then I have been having numerous serial, very vivid "busting paradigm" dreams about ending old ways of life.

In the dreams I am creating new endings to countless old dramas in my life and creating new endings to countless old dramas for humanity. Within these new ending dreams I am literally breaking paradigms about judgment, gender, family, relationships, inequality, and so on. In some dreams I am busting these paradigms physically, like with a hammer, to the point of horrific violence. At other times I am doing so emotionally, like manipulating an old scenario to re-work it to a better, though sort of ill-gotten result. In every single dream I am shocked at what I am willing to do to break the "routine" of past paradigms. In not a single dream have I brought about a new ending gently, yet in every single dream the end result is one of freedom, compassion and equality.

I must admit I feel deeply relieved having done this work; I feel thoroughly cleansed in some way. But I am also a little appalled at what my mind is capable of in terms of the brutality with which I have been making these changes.

The emotions in these dreams feel powerfully egoic, like a tantrum of "I have had enough!" and the result is everything from explosive rage to pitiful selfishness. But the intent feels spiritual, like the means to releasing all this pent up emotion justifies the ends of equanimity and wisdom.

I truly do not subscribe to the idea of having to do battle in order for good to overcome evil, and I truly do not believe conflict is necessary to gain peace. In processing these experiences it feels like I am ridding myself (and my contributions to humanity) of what I have been taught are old paradigms AND what I have been taught are the ways to "conquer" these old paradigms. Because the intent feels spiritual and the actions feel egoic, perhaps I have finally arrived at the point on the bridge between Divine and physical realms where Ego has agreed to work together with Love. If this is the case I will be very happy if my Ego really has had enough.

Chapter 44

I have been back at Thosamling now for two months and barely recognize the person I was when I arrived. I was raggedly worn down after spending eighteen months in another difficult but necessary demolition derby phase of this journey, running into a trove of old issues over and over again. I have been forced to look with sober honesty at more of what the world "out there" had been triggering in me, and to examine the true intentions behind every decision, the feelings beneath every reaction and the lessons in every situation. But this time I have been able to look at all these difficulties against the backdrop of what I know spiritually to steadily build my courage and strength back up and genuinely transmute old pain, insecurities and fears compassionately into love.

I have also been able to do this work in the continued company of that formless, transparent spirit – but on a much more personal level. I recognized the spirit's distinctly familiar energy one evening when I entered the room of a spunky fellow resident I barely knew. I went there to help her bandage a cut she suffered in a fall, and as soon as I stepped over the threshold I knew something was different. The woman was unmistakably part of the spirit that has been cheering me on for months. But I said nothing to her since we did not know each other well and she knew nothing of my story. A few days later the woman happened to be helping a nun with a computer problem and the two came together to my room for assistance. While we were all chatting, I said something that caught the woman delightfully off guard. She laughed joyfully, then playfully tousled my hair and kissed the top of my head. We are now friends. Or perhaps reacquainted old friends.

With every step of this arduous journey, whether graceful or stumbling, and with continual help from a vast array of sources, I have been able to embody more and more of the words I have been given from God, Jesus, Buddha and others who are part of the collective Christ consciousness that I know is fast returning to the human experience. As I resurrect my own life, letting old mental constructs of fear and conflict die and letting heart-founded universal truth and Love rise, I become more of who I really Am – more of The Message of the resurrected Christ. This is my life purpose. This is the journey I am to understand and to help others understand, and writing this book has been an important step toward that objective for me and hopefully will be for others. I will continue on this journey now diligently, willingly and slowly, slowly until I succeed. For I have been assured I cannot fail.

As I write these last words of Part Two, I have tears of what feels like lifelong relief in my eyes. I wrote Part Three in one hour under the guidance of Jesus more than a year ago. Just this moment in writing the above paragraph I was "told" to go to Part Three now and add at the beginning: These are the words that come from the place of perfect love and wisdom.

176

Chapter 45

I am awakened from a deep sleep at 4:24 AM with a powerful call to sit up and receive the following message:

"The time has come."

Here I see a veil around Earth lift and the "air" clear for all, then the message continues:

"For those who Know – those whose light will become visible to others – you have a responsibility now. Speak only your Truth of Love and nothing more [meaning do not embellish and trust your ability to speak from your higher Self]. This is very important, for this is the integrity of Light."

Here I see the "leaving behind" of many outdated physical/mental/emotional bodies and new forms take their place, then the message continues:

"You are the Way. Understand with all your being that you Know this and the Way will be seen by others. Others will then awaken to their own choices."

I watch now as a massive gathering of countless Divine beings – masters, archangels, angels, etc. – come together throughout the cosmos. They all watch in jubilant celebration as individual bodies of light begin to illuminate one by one around planet Earth.

Part 3

*These are the words that come from the place
of perfect love and wisdom.
These are the words to BE, from the heart.
These are the words to be taken in and lived.*

~Jesus

I Am

I Am the Way of Love, the Truth of Love and the luminous Light of Love.

Where the rhythm of awareness beats in the heart, I Am Christ.

Where trust prevails and fear is no more, I Am Christ.

I Am pure compassion, kindness, and wisdom.

I Am absolute peace and love.

I Am all possibility.

I Am all.

I Am.

I Am Within

For each, I am found in the shell of no other. Where there is unity with the Love within, I Am.

I Am the soothingly rich depth of the quiet mind and the vast knowing flowing through the heart. When the mind and heart reconcile to the truth of oneness, I Am.

No scripture or sermon is necessary to live according to Love. Every heart knows the way. The very current pulsing through every heart is Love, and in Love there is no other admonition than to BE Love. I Am this Love.

I Am Equality

I Am the Truth that all are equal, for all are One. Equality does not mean conformity. All aspects of life are by their very nature unique aspects of Love that are equally precious and beloved. All give life to Love and Love gives life to All.

I speak as Love beneath the sounds of fear and judgment. I Am the Truth that judgment is in direct opposition to unconditional Love. Where unconditional Love is opposed, there is suffering. Where unconditional Love flourishes, I Am.

Where the roots of conflict are pulled up and seeds of unity are planted, I Am.

I Am Forgiveness

I Am the recognition that there is nothing to forgive.

I Am above and below no other and therefore make no judgment of another's rightness or wrongness. I Am the understanding that there is nothing to be right or wrong about. There simply *is* without meaning. Meaning is assigned in the mind of Man alone. I Am the true compassionate understanding behind the false façade of meaning.

I Am Intention

I Am the intention of Love.

I Am the intention behind every thought to BE the goodness of Love.

I Am the intention of compassion and kindness behind every word and deed.

I Am the intention to BE Love.

I Am Reverence

I Am that which reveres no one but Love, and even that in gratitude alone.

I Am the BE-ing of God's life, which is Love, and all around and within me are equally Love.

I Am Commerce and Community

I Am the currency of compassion and caring.

I Am the exchange of Love for Love.

I Am the Divine tender of joy, sustenance, experience and support.

I Am the thrill of nurturance, the passion of empathy, the undying devotion to Love in All.

I Am that which releases the shackles of slavery and exploitation. I Am that which heals blindness to one's own worth, unleashes one's own potential and in eternal freedom allows one to live according to one's own joyful expression of Love.

I Am Passion

I Am the passionate Love within me. I Am the passionate Love for me.

I Am the passionate heralding of my spirit and soul equal to that of all, which is equal to Love.

I Am the passionate celebration and embrace of all life equally, for all life is wondrous expression of Love.

I Am Gratitude

Above all, I Am gratitude beyond compare for the miracle of all life, for life is Love living itself.

I Am Now

All the endless interpretations of my past are moot. Right now is all that matters. There is nothing in my evolution that is more important than this moment. I Am Here. I Am Now.

What the world thinks of me – any version of me – based on the past is irrelevant. The past separates me from the present and is therefore of no use. I am only to be known *now*; there is no other way.

Final words

All will know me. At first some will be scared for they do not understand what is happening. Then they will be surprised when they realize what is at hand. Then they will know a peace and happiness they have never known. They will know me, Christ.

There is *great* love coming... like a great tidal wave... like the force of a thousand winds. It is unstoppable.

You should welcome it when it comes.

.

Author's Note

The visions and insights included in this book were chosen because their content helped me unfold my story in the most effective and least confusing way. With the exception of the initial events with Sue, all mystical events mentioned happened between early 2011 and early 2014. Some of these events happened in seemingly random order, so I placed them in a sequence I thought would be easiest for others to follow. I did not include every vision or insight I have experienced nor did I describe every event in its entirety. As Garje Khamtrul Rinpoche advised, at this point I am only sharing what I think people can hear, and what I have chosen to share feels right on every level. I painstakingly made every attempt to maintain content accuracy using as reference written documentation I usually make after each event.

As much as possible, I avoided personal narration or interpretation of any information provided by God, Jesus or Buddha. Anything I say I "know" I actually embodied or gleaned directly from metaphysical insight. It became clear to me when I began this manuscript that all I was supposed to do was allow events to speak for themselves.

Narrative chapters in Part Two are based either on a blog I kept to journal my first stay in India or on personal communications with friends and family. I maintained the integrity of all original materials, editing most minimally if at all, however a few were edited more extensively to present information in a cleaner and clearer manner than I had achieved in my awkward early attempts to write about what I know.

I made a deliberate choice not to disclose many details of my childhood or life prior to my suicide attempt, including specifics of the series of catastrophes that led to the collapse of my "normal" life. I also chose not to include a great deal of information about my family, friends or private relationships other than brief mention for contextual purposes.

I omitted this information in order to maintain focus on the present moment relationship I had to have with myself so as to have a relationship with God, Jesus and Buddha. I am aware that our storytelling culture dictates that we usually develop characters in a broad context of external influences against backdrops of the past. But I am also aware that in doing this when writing about ourselves we select which narratives about our past define our character and thereby narrow our whole truth to mere slivers, dismissing the countless ways every other influence led us along our winding paths and made us behave and think the way we do. This then narrows our gratitude and appreciation for all we have been and all we have become.

It is not possible to express all that I am grateful for and appreciative of in my life. There just aren't enough words or ways to do it because ultimately every moment led me to God, Jesus, Buddha, the angels and my own divinity. So my aim was not to use my unique life puzzle pieces to put together my version of an age-old story about overcoming hardships. My aim was to share a true journey of self-acceptance, resurrection and enlightenment solely using events I feel were most pertinent to my spiritual evolution.

About the words 'resurrection' and 'enlightenment': these are just words. Like all other words they were created by humans, have been translated from other words that were created by humans, and are subject to endless interpretations of meaning and appropriate use. I intend them respectfully and use them with this meaning: I rose from certain death to new life and have seen truths of the universe directly through God, Jesus and Buddha.

Finally, I mention in Chapter Two that I was having visions and insights for several years before the mystical experiences became only about spiritual matters. Again, I omitted details about these events so as not to distract from the main storyline. However, these events were an indicator that I had a window into ways of seeing that I did not yet understand. The events included episodes of precisely accurate clairvoyance, sightings of translucent spirits, "becoming" someone else just before I met them, and several movie-like "parallel life" episodes where I was in the lives of other people in different eras while also still going about my normal day. I had no idea what these experiences were about and did not try at that time to find out why or how I was having them.

Images of Akiane Kramerik's work are provided by Akiane Gallery. Other than these images, all work herein was created by and is owned by me. Any and all of my work may be shared with the stipulation that no changes are made to wording or context and no false representation is made of authorship, ownership or individuals and experiences mentioned.

Acknowledgements

My deepest thanks first and foremost to God, Jesus, Buddha, Archangel Michael and all other Divine beings that guide me, trust me and keep me company. I love you with everything I Am. May this work bring you joy, and may these WORDS be of humble assistance in universal efforts to end to suffering for all beings.

I wrote the final words of this manuscript exactly three years and one day after I woke up from my failed suicide attempt. The path that took me out of despair and into this publication has been long, winding, confusing, challenging, enchanting, enriching and most all, healing. Through it all I have been blessed with friends and family who have loved me and supported me in meaningful ways, from care packages and "you can do it!" messages to a shoulder to cry on and a bed to sleep in. The powerhouse heroes include Heather Phillips, the one person who has known my secret from the beginning and who has been waiting for this day as long as I have; my eternally-beloved siblings, Marva and Marvin, and their families, for traveling beside me in this life with laughter and love; my beloved father, Marvin Reed Sr., for being the greatest earth-bound teacher of forgiveness and unconditional love; Sue Lanier for opening the spiritual gates; Traci Dinwiddie, Barbara Glynn, Reese J., Nancy M. and Mary W. for being inspirational strongholds; Kerry Beach for his love, his incredible home stretch contributions, and boundless confidence in my work; Lisa Dewey for invaluable and memorable home stretch cheerleading; and my entire Front Porch family for their blessedly awesome company (especially invested and influential lovelies Linda Andersson, Svetla Atanasova, Elisabeth Arellano, Joany B., Beatriz Bravo, Dayna Carlson, Elena Delamora, Debra Tulimiero Duffield, Connie Dunning and her mother Kathy Holmes, Maureen Eastty, Carla Espinoza, Corinne Gans, Veronique Gistang, Adriana Gonzalez, Darcy Harris, Jody Harris, Chris Hirsch, Nancy Hermann, Tricia Howe, Chris Kovacs, Shelli Larkin, Lorraine Lasala, Janet Luallen, Maggy M., Arlene Mengel, Stephanie Meyer, Simone Moura, Sarah Read, Pam Robinson, Tiara Sinha Roy, Melissa Sendelbach, D'Ann Townsend, Linda Tysinger, Bernadette van Essen, Eberhardt van Gould, Martina Vasileva and Veerle Vyncke). Also of significant influence and encouragement were Mudita Badhwar and her parents Deepak and Kangan, Jane Clark, Jill Renee Feeler, Garje Khamtrul Rinpoche, His Holiness the 14th Dalai Lama, His Holiness the 17th Karmapa, Cynthea Gillespie Kinnaman, Mozelle Kunkel, Barbara Lang, Barbara Lipton, Dr. Joe Mancini, Kay Pfaltz, kindred spirits at Platinum Age Ground Crew, Jackie Powers, Annig Raley, Rinchen, and all others whose words or actions inspired me and validated the importance of my efforts along the way. Thank you, thank you, one and all.

Thanks also to Judy Kern, whose encouraging courtesy review of an early, unfinished draft of this manuscript helped strengthen my voice.

Special thanks and a deep bow of love to Venerable Tenzin Sangmo and the staff of Thosamling for giving me a safe, embracing and beautiful place to BE. I am crazy about all of you. Thanks, too, to Yogesh for leading me to

Thosamling and to all the fellow nunnery residents who inspired me with their own peace-driven journeys.

Finally, this story would not have been possible without Dr. Rudy Bauer and Margery Silverton. There will never be enough words to express the fullness of my gratitude for their belief in me and for their wise guidance.